# The Hidden
# Beauty
# of the Shema

# The Hidden
# Beauty
# of the Shema

Lisa Aiken, Ph.D.

TARGUM/FELDHEIM

*First published 1997*
Copyright © 1997 by Lisa Aiken
ISBN 1-56871-115-8

Published by:
**Targum Press, Inc.**
22700 W. Eleven Mile Rd.
Southfield, MI 48034

Distributed by:
**Feldheim Publishers**
200 Airport Executive Park
Nanuet, NY 10954

Distributed in Israel by:
**Targum Press Ltd.**
POB 43170
Jerusalem 91430

*Printed in Israel*

**Aish HaTorah**
College of Jewish Studies

Jerusalem, 3 Adar I, 5757 (February 10, 1997)

I have received the book *The Hidden Beauty of the Shema* by Dr. Lisa Aiken. Once again Dr. Aiken has provided the English-speaking Torah community with a quality work.

She ably weaves together the laws and *hashkafah* of the Shema, thereby creating a synthesis of Torah.

This book will be of value, both to the Torah scholar and beginner alike.

It is my prayer that the great truth of the Shema permeate the entire Jewish nation, *"When you are at home, when you are traveling along the road, when you lie down, or when you arise,"* that the idea of the Shema truly surround us in our gates and homes, in our hearts and minds.

May this book serve as an impetus in the transformation of this command and prayer into a reality.

May the Al-Mighty bless Dr. Aiken with many more years of health and productivity.

Rabbi Noah Weinberg
Rosh HaYeshiva
Aish HaTorah

NEVE·YERUSHALAYIM

ג ו ה · ' ר ו ש ל י ם

Lisa Aiken's book on Shema will, God willing, be another contribution of inestimable value to her fellow Jew. As with her other books, her lucid and honest presentation of material all too often inaccessible to the English-speaking reader will not only fill a gap in information, but may very well change lives.

The Torah wisdom she absorbed from Rabbi Kirzner, זצ״ל, fills every page with light. May she be worthy of providing us with still more.

Sincerely,

Tziporah Heller

# Dedication

This book is dedicated to Batya שתח׳.
May you bring divine light into others' lives as you have brought it into mine.

# Table of Contents

# Acknowledgments

I am indebted to Rabbi Dovid Gottlieb, Ph.D., for carefully reviewing this manuscript and making many helpful suggestions for improving it. I thank him from the bottom of my heart.

I also wish to express my appreciation to Rebbetzin Tzippora Heller for her suggestions about publishing this book.

As always, my heartfelt thanks to Ira Michaels for his incisive and important comments. His objective criticism has been invaluable.

# Foreword

Jews say two especially important prayers every day: the Shema and the *Amidah*. We fulfill the biblical commandment (mitzvah) to say the Shema every morning and evening when we say its first verse, "Hear, Israel, the Lord is our God, the Lord is One." The rabbis, however, required us to add three additional paragraphs, drawn from the books of Deuteronomy and Numbers.[1] Besides our reciting the Shema daily, we also say it before going to sleep, over a baby boy the night before his ritual circumcision (brit milah), and before we die.

The commandments to which the Shema refers — tefillin (leather boxes containing parchments that are put on a man's head and arm), mezuzah (a parchment with Torah verses that we put on our doorposts), tzitzit (fringes that are put on a four-cornered garment), and remembering the Exodus from Egypt — are also part of our daily lives. Thus, the Shema literally accompanies us from cradle to grave.

The Minchat Chinuch explains why the Shema and its mitzvot (commandments) "surround" us: People tend to be drawn to materialism and give in to their lusts by following foolish, worldly pleasures. We need constant reminders that we are part of God's Cabinet and have responsibilities to Him. Without these reminders, we can't keep focused on what God put us here to do. His lovingkindness determined that we should say the Shema twice a day to help us stay on track spiritually.[2]

The general purpose of any mitzvah is to preserve and heighten our spiritual wholesomeness and to attach us to God. Saying the Shema reminds us that our thoughts, speech, and actions affect the entire universe.[3] That, in turn, encourages us to live with ongoing devotion and fervor in our service to the Almighty. The Shema also refocuses us at least twice a day so that we are not derailed by constant exposure to forces that negate our spirituality.

The Shema can help us regain our spiritual bearings and infuse us with tremendous spiritual energy only if we appreciate and concentrate on what we are saying. This book was designed to help us do that.

Given that the Shema is such an important daily prayer, and that it has such profound spiritual effects, it is surprising that English Judaica has largely neglected it. The present work is an attempt to fill this gap.

This book incorporates ideas from Rabbi Moshe Chaim Luzzatto's writings about the Shema in *The Way of God*, and was strongly influenced by my understanding of the teachings of Rabbi Yitzchok Kirzner, zt"l, on this subject. At times, I have borrowed ideas that I heard from Rabbis Aryeh Kaplan, zt"l, and Uziel Milevsky, zt"l. I hope that these ideas will inspire others as they did me.

*Lisa Aiken, Ph.D.*

## Notes

1. Many rabbis maintain that saying the entire first paragraph of the Shema is biblically mandated. Some even maintain that the same applies to the second paragraph.

2. Women are not required to say the Shema twice a day, inasmuch as it is a time-bound commandment from which they are exempt. Nevertheless, many contemporary rabbis recommend that women say it, and many women do so regularly.

3. *Sefer HaChinuch*, mitzvah 421. Men evidently need these reminders more than women. Women are neither required to say the Shema nor must they wear tzitzit and tefillin. However, should women choose to say the Shema, they can reap the same benefits from it that men do.

# Preface

During World War II, countless Jewish parents gave their precious children to Christian neighbors and orphanages in the hope that the latter would provide safe havens for them. The parents expected that they, or their relatives, would take these children back if they survived the war.

The few parents who did not perish in the Holocaust, and were able to reclaim their children, often faced another horror. While the parents had summoned the strength to survive the slave labor and death camps, or had hidden out for years, those who took their children were busy teaching them to love Christianity, and to hate Jews and Judaism.

To add insult to injury, many Jewish children who were taken in by Christian orphanages, convents, and the like, had no parents or close relatives left after the Holocaust. When rabbis or distant relatives finally tracked down many of these children, the priests and nuns who had been their caretakers insisted that no children from Jewish homes were in their institutions. Thus, countless Jewish children were not only stripped of their entire families, they were also stripped of their souls.

In May, 1945, Rabbi Eliezer Silver from the United States and Dayan Grunfeld from England were sent as chaplains to liberate some of the death camps. While there, they were told that many Jewish children had been placed in a monastery in Alsace-Lorraine. The rabbis went there to reclaim them.

When they approached the priest in charge, they asked that the Jewish children be released into the rabbis' care.

"I'm sorry," the priest responded, "but there is no way of knowing which children here came from Jewish families. You must have documentation if you wish me to do what you ask."

Of course, the kind of documentation that the priest wanted was unobtainable at the end of the war. The rabbis asked to see the list of names of children who were in the monastery. As the rabbis read the list, they pointed to those that belonged to Jewish children.

"I'm sorry," the priest insisted, "but the names that you pointed to could be either Jewish or Gentile. Miller is a German name, and Markovich is a Russian name, and Swersky is a Polish name. You can't prove that these are Jewish children. If you can't prove which children are Jewish, and do it very quickly, you will have to leave."

One of the rabbis had a brilliant idea. "We'd like to come back again this evening when you are putting the children to sleep." The priest reluctantly agreed.

That evening the rabbis came to the dormitory, where row upon row of little beds were arranged. The children, many of whom had been in the monastery since the war started in 1939, were going to sleep. The rabbis walked through the  aisles of beds, calling out, "Shema, Yisrael,

Hashem Elokeinu, Hashem Echad!" ("Hear, Jewish people, the Lord is our God, the Lord is One!")

One by one, children burst into tears and shrieked, "Mommy!" "Maman!" "Momma!" "Mamushka!" in each of their native tongues.

The priest had succeeded in teaching these precious Jewish souls about the Trinity, the New Testament, and the Christian savior. Each child knew how to say Mass. But the priest did not succeed in erasing these children's memories of their Jewish mothers — now murdered — putting them to bed every night with the Shema on their lips.

(My thanks to Miriam Swerdlov for relating this story to me.)

# The Shema

(יָחִיד אוֹמֵר: אֵל מֶלֶךְ נֶאֱמָן)

(God is a faithful King.)

שְׁמַע | יִשְׂרָאֵל, יְיָ | אֱלֹהֵינוּ, יְיָ | אֶחָד:

Hear, Israel, the Lord is our God, the Lord is One.[1]

בָּרוּךְ שֵׁם כְּבוֹד מַלְכוּתוֹ לְעוֹלָם וָעֶד.

Blessed is the Name of His glorious kingdom forever
and ever.

וְאָהַבְתָּ אֵת יְיָ | אֱלֹהֶיךָ, בְּכָל-לְבָבְךָ, וּבְכָל-נַפְשְׁךָ, וּבְכָל-מְאֹדֶךָ.
וְהָיוּ הַדְּבָרִים הָאֵלֶּה, אֲשֶׁר | אָנֹכִי מְצַוְּךָ הַיּוֹם, עַל-לְבָבֶךָ:
וְשִׁנַּנְתָּם לְבָנֶיךָ, וְדִבַּרְתָּ בָּם בְּשִׁבְתְּךָ בְּבֵיתֶךָ, וּבְלֶכְתְּךָ בַדֶּרֶךְ
וּבְשָׁכְבְּךָ, וּבְקוּמֶךָ. וּקְשַׁרְתָּם לְאוֹת | עַל-יָדֶךָ, וְהָיוּ לְטֹטָפֹת בֵּין |
עֵינֶיךָ, וּכְתַבְתָּם | עַל מְזֻזֹת בֵּיתֶךָ וּבִשְׁעָרֶיךָ:

And you should love the Lord your God with all of your
heart, and with all of your soul, and with all of your resources.
And these words that I command you today should be on
your heart. And you should teach them to your children, and

speak of them when you sit in your house, and when you
go on the way, and when you lie down, and when you rise
up. And you should bind them as a sign on your hand, and
they should be tefillin between your eyes. And write them
on the doorposts of your house and in your gates.[2]

וְהָיָה אִם-שָׁמֹעַ תִּשְׁמְעוּ אֶל-מִצְוֹתַי, אֲשֶׁר l אָנֹכִי מְצַוֶּה l אֶתְכֶם
הַיּוֹם, לְאַהֲבָה אֶת יְיָ l אֱלֹהֵיכֶם, וּלְעָבְדוֹ בְּכָל-לְבַבְכֶם וּבְכָל
נַפְשְׁכֶם. וְנָתַתִּי מְטַר-אַרְצְכֶם בְּעִתּוֹ, יוֹרֶה וּמַלְקוֹשׁ, וְאָסַפְתָּ
דְגָנֶךָ וְתִירֹשְׁךָ וְיִצְהָרֶךָ. וְנָתַתִּי l עֵשֶׂב l בְּשָׂדְךָ לִבְהֶמְתֶּךָ, וְאָכַלְתָּ
וְשָׂבָעְתָּ. הִשָּׁמְרוּ לָכֶם פֶּן-יִפְתֶּה לְבַבְכֶם, וְסַרְתֶּם וַעֲבַדְתֶּם l
אֱלֹהִים l אֲחֵרִים וְהִשְׁתַּחֲוִיתֶם לָהֶם. וְחָרָה l אַף-יְיָ בָּכֶם, וְעָצַר l
אֶת-הַשָּׁמַיִם וְלֹא-יִהְיֶה מָטָר, וְהָאֲדָמָה לֹא תִתֵּן אֶת-יְבוּלָהּ
וַאֲבַדְתֶּם l מְהֵרָה מֵעַל הָאָרֶץ הַטֹּבָה l אֲשֶׁר l יְיָ נֹתֵן לָכֶם:
וְשַׂמְתֶּם l אֶת דְּבָרַי l אֵלֶּה עַל-לְבַבְכֶם וְעַל-נַפְשְׁכֶם וּקְשַׁרְתֶּם l
אֹתָם לְאוֹת l עַל-יֶדְכֶם, וְהָיוּ לְטוֹטָפֹת בֵּין l עֵינֵיכֶם: וְלִמַּדְתֶּם l
אֹתָם l אֶת-בְּנֵיכֶם, לְדַבֵּר בָּם, בְּשִׁבְתְּךָ בְּבֵיתֶךָ, וּבְלֶכְתְּךָ בַדֶּרֶךְ,
וּבְשָׁכְבְּךָ וּבְקוּמֶךָ: וּכְתַבְתָּם l עַל-מְזוּזוֹת בֵּיתֶךָ וּבִשְׁעָרֶיךָ: לְמַעַן
l יִרְבּוּ l יְמֵיכֶם וִימֵי בְנֵיכֶם עַל הָאֲדָמָה l אֲשֶׁר l נִשְׁבַּע l יְיָ
לַאֲבֹתֵיכֶם לָתֵת לָהֶם, כִּימֵי הַשָּׁמַיִם l עַל-הָאָרֶץ:

And it shall be, if you listen carefully to My mitzvot that
I command you today, to love the Lord your God and to
serve Him with all of your heart and with all of your soul,
then I will give the rain for your land in its proper time,
the early and the late rains, and you will gather in your
grain, your wine, and your oil. And I will give grass in your
fields for your cattle, and you will eat and be satisfied.
Watch yourselves, lest your hearts seduce you, and you go
astray and serve strange gods, and bow down to them. And
the Lord will be angry with you, and will hold back the
heavens, and there will not be rain, and the earth will not
give its produce, and you will quickly be lost from the good

land that the Lord gives you. And you should put these words on your hearts and on your souls, and bind them as a sign on your hand, and they should be tefillin between your eyes. And you should teach them to your children, and speak of them when you sit in your house, and when you go on the way, and when you lie down, and when you rise up. And write them on the doorposts of your house and in your gates. In order that your days, and the days of your children, be many upon the land that the Lord swore to your forefathers to give them, like the days of the heavens on the earth.[3]

וַיֹּאמֶר ו יְיָ ו אֶל־מֹשֶׁה לֵּאמֹר: דַּבֵּר ו אֶל־בְּנֵי ו יִשְׂרָאֵל וְאָמַרְתָּ אֲלֵהֶם: וְעָשׂוּ לָהֶם צִיצִת עַל־כַּנְפֵי בִגְדֵיהֶם לְדֹרֹתָם, וְנָתְנוּ ו עַל־ צִיצִת הַכָּנָף פְּתִיל תְּכֵלֶת. וְהָיָה לָכֶם לְצִיצִת, וּרְאִיתֶם ו אֹתוֹ וּזְכַרְתֶּם ו אֶת־כָּל־מִצְוֹת ו יְיָ, וַעֲשִׂיתֶם ו אֹתָם, וְלֹא תָתוּרוּ ו אַחֲרֵי לְבַבְכֶם וְאַחֲרֵי ו עֵינֵיכֶם, אֲשֶׁר־אַתֶּם זֹנִים ו אַחֲרֵיהֶם: לְמַעַן תִּזְכְּרוּ וַעֲשִׂיתֶם ו אֶת־כָּל־מִצְוֹתָי, וִהְיִיתֶם קְדֹשִׁים לֵאלֹהֵיכֶם: אֲנִי יְיָ ו אֱלֹהֵיכֶם, אֲשֶׁר הוֹצֵאתִי ו אֶתְכֶם ו מֵאֶרֶץ מִצְרַיִם, לִהְיוֹת לָכֶם לֵאלֹהִים, אֲנִי ו יְיָ ו אֱלֹהֵיכֶם:

And the Lord spoke to Moses, saying: Speak to the children of Israel, and tell them to make themselves fringes (tzitzit) on the corners of their garments for all their generations; and they should put a blue strand on the corner fringe. And you will have tzitzit, and you shall see them, and you will remember all of the Lord's commandments, and do them. And you shall not stray after your hearts and after your eyes, that you lust after, so that you will remember and do all of My commandments, and be holy to your God. I am the Lord your God who brought you out of the land of Egypt to be your God. I am the Lord your God [in truth].[4]

## *Notes*

1. Deuteronomy 6:4.
2. Ibid. 6:5–9.
3. Ibid. 11:13–21.
4. Numbers 15:37–41.

# Introduction

The essence of the Shema is our acknowledging God's unity and uniqueness and accepting our obligation to do His commandments. The Shema continually reminds us that we are subjects of a great and awesome King, who wants us to act, think, and speak in ways that show our appreciation for the fact that everything we do affects the entire world.

We are supposed to say the Shema at least twice a day, in the morning and at night.[1] If we start and end our day with a sense of God's Unity, Kingdom, and providence over us, we will take seriously the idea that He is always watching us and taking into account everything we do. That awareness will keep us from living mindlessly or frivolously, and prevent us from thinking that we can hide our immorality from Him.

Two people who love each other don't have to be together at every moment. But if one wants to be rid of the other much of the time, they will soon become estranged.

This same idea applies to us and God. We often want Him to leave us alone during the day and only be part of our lives when we pray or do religious rituals. We can't feel very close to Him if we live this way.

It is natural to find "too much" religiosity oppressive if we do mitzvot mechanically, or see them merely as "brownie points" to be accumulated. The true purpose of life is to develop our relationship with the Almighty such that we experience the exquisite spiritual pleasure of closeness to Him. That surpasses all other pleasures, and we create receptivity to it every time that we do a mitzvah with the right frame of mind.

By appreciating how everything we do can draw us closer to our Creator, by continually relating to Him in every part of our lives, and by doing His commandments, we can enjoy His love and nearness. Whenever we draw Him out of hiding in our daily lives, we make Him more apparent to ourselves and to others.

We need to say the Shema twice a day because it serves a critical spiritual function. It affirms our belief in one God who cares about, and is always involved in, the details of our personal lives. It also shows that we accept religious responsibilities. Yet there is also more to the Shema than this. We will plumb its depths by first exploring the basic philosophical concepts that underlie it.

### Notes

1. The morning Shema is said during the first quarter of the day. It may be said before sunrise, provided it is light enough to (visually) recognize a friend six feet away.

   The Jewish day is divided into twelve parts, or "seasonal hours," starting at sunrise and ending at sunset. Thus, the length of a seasonal hour is usually more or less than 60 minutes, depending upon the time of year. In the summer, daylight might last 16 hours. Dividing that by 12 results in

80-minute seasonal hours. In winter, there may be only 9 hours of daylight, making each "hour" only 45 minutes long.

The first quarter of the day starts at sunrise and ends when three seasonal hours have elapsed. In winter, if the sun rises at 7:15, the morning Shema might be read until 9:30 A.M. In summer, if the sun rises at 4:30, it might be read only until 8:30 A.M.

The evening Shema may be said from the time that three stars appear (approximately 42 minutes after sunset) until dawn the next day, although it is preferable to read it before midnight. The Talmudic Sages recommended not waiting until dawn because they were concerned that people would take an evening nap, thinking that they had plenty of time to say the Shema, then oversleep and wake up after sunrise. (These laws are discussed in *Berachot* 10b.)

# 1
## God's Unity and Uniqueness

God created an incredibly complex, yet orderly, world that has both physical and spiritual elements in it. Everything physical has a spiritual purpose, yet the world tends to function according to the laws of nature. Nature, however, does not have its own, independent existence, but depends upon God's will. The Almighty both created nature and determines how it functions moment by moment, so that the world will reach His spiritual goals for it.

People who are not spiritually sensitized don't see the divine will fueling nature. They see only Nature. At best, they believe that God created the world, then let it evolve totally on its own. Judaism teaches that our Creator runs the world, and always has. It didn't get here on its own, nor do forces other than the Master of the Universe ultimately control it. He does this with a creativity and power that are uniquely His. No one and no other forces are comparable to Him, and nothing exists or functions without His allowing it to do so.[1] God oversees and rules all other forces in the universe such that nature and human beings necessarily have less power than He does.

In His goodness, He lets us feel powerful and creative, but we can't create the way He does. We can only take existing materials, put them together, and produce something that lasts a long time. If we want a table, we cut some pieces of wood, bolt them together, and make a piece of furniture that hopefully lasts for a few hundred years.

By contrast, God created *ex nihilo*, from nothing. Before He started creating the world, nothing existed except Him. Since there were initially no raw materials, He created the building blocks of the universe by willing them to exist. The Torah expresses this by saying in the Creation story, "And God said, 'Let there be light, and there was light.' "[2] "And God said, 'Let there be a firmament in the midst of the waters...' and it was so."[3] "And God said, 'Let there be lights in the firmament...,' "[4] and so on.

God not only created the world by willing things to exist, but the world only continues to exist to the extent that He wills it. We take for granted that the sun will rise tomorrow because it rose today, and has risen since the dawn of time. We assume that our homes and possessions will not suddenly disappear, because material objects don't usually dematerialize. We assume that time will continue marching on because it has done so for as long as human beings have been alive. But if our Creator stopped willing anything to be here, it would immediately revert to nothingness. The entire world, and time, could disappear in an instant! (Even time is a creation.) The fact that something exists tells us that God wills it to be here.

This is a difficult idea to conceptualize because it flies in the face of what we know about the physical world. In our experience, either something is or it isn't. Its continued existence seems to depend upon the laws of nature, rather than divine will.

This concept is also hard to understand because we are limited. We have limited intelligence, limited abilities, and limited memory. Once we make something, we might forget about it. And if we try to keep track of too many things at once, we can't. We may be able to remember ten things that need our supervision, but keeping 10,000 matters in mind that require immediate attention is completely beyond our ability.

On the other hand, God is an infinite, perfect Being. This is part of what we mean when we say that He is One. As such, He has no limitations of intelligence, ability, or memory. He does not forget anything that He created, and is consequently constantly mindful of every creature and creation in His universe. Being completely aware of the thoughts, needs, and deeds of five billion people is no different to Him than doing the same for five people. His ability to run His world doesn't get stretched thin by increasing numbers or complexity. His infinity is always greater than the finite number of creations and creatures that He made, no matter how big that finite number is.

Human beings can be aware of, forget about, or destroy things that we make. The Almighty never forgets about His creations. He only chooses to sustain or destroy them by willing or not willing them to exist. We express this concept in our morning prayers by saying that God "renews, in His goodness, every day, constantly, the act of Creation." Everything exists only by His ongoing wish that it do so.

It is God's will that the world run according to the laws of nature whenever possible, but there are times when He deems it necessary to operate supernaturally. For example, He does this when He makes obvious miracles. At those times when He wants nature to change, He simply alters His will, and nature automatically changes.

## The Role of Evil

God did not create anything physical as an end in itself. He made everything in the world to serve spiritual purposes. For example, His entire reason for creating the world was so that people would have a realm within which we could earn His goodness by following His will while being challenged to do otherwise.[5] Rather than being welfare recipients who get good things from God regardless of what we do, He wanted us to be tempted not to do His bidding, then overcome those challenges. That makes the ultimate reward that we get for our efforts much more meaningful than if we had never worked hard to get what we achieve.

The ultimate goodness that we get as a reward is the intimate, eternal relationship that our soul enjoys with the Almighty in the afterlife. We can only truly appreciate that reward after spending a lifetime choosing spirituality over the sensual and material allures of this world.

As part of His plan, God determined during Creation how evil would function throughout history. He wanted it to challenge us on a daily basis to go against His will, yet also intended it eventually to reveal goodness. He made wrongdoing appealing by giving us a negative inclination (known as the *yetzer hara*) that urges us to violate His wishes. At the same time, He gave us the wherewithal to overcome temptations by giving us a good inclination (known as the *yetzer hatov*).[6] When we conquer our drive to disobey God and reject immoral choices, we automatically transform negativity into positive spiritual energy. The spiritual good that we create by destroying negativity is proportional to how strong the challenge is. Conquering our passions and channeling them to serve God turns us into masters of our destinies and gives us true worth.

The world's negativity and challenges do not happen randomly. Rather, each instance occurs according to an intricate divine plan that allows positive things to happen in the end. Only God's tremendous wisdom can fathom exactly what form each type of negativity should take, when it should occur, how it should come into each of our lives, and how we should deal with it. Only His infinite knowledge can comprehend how each instance of negativity, from the beginning of time until the Messianic era, will eventually lead to good.[7]

All negativity will disappear during the Messianic era because negativity is artificial and ephemeral, while goodness is eternal. When ultimate truth emerges at the end of time, goodness will totally replace evil. The moment that truth becomes so compelling that everyone follows it, negativity will lose all of its strength.

In the Messianic era, evil will be destroyed, but not by intergalactic warfare. Evil will automatically stop when everyone clearly sees God's infinite power and presence, partly revealed through miracles that will happen then. Once people see the futility of disobeying God, no one will waste his energies and talents doing it. Evil will disappear because the wrong choices will no longer have any allure.

In the Messianic era, everyone will proclaim, "I know without a shadow of a doubt that there is one God." They will enjoy the pinnacle of blessing inherent in realizing that the Almighty is the only true existence.

## Relating to Negativity

It is hard for most people to accept that God deliberately allows evil, that He is the Master of a world where life seems unfair and injustice abounds. If we did not have compelling reasons to believe in a Torah that teaches that God *is* fair, good, and runs the world, we would believe the opposite because that is what we see and experience. Torah lets us see our material world not as reality, but as a confusion of reality.

Truth and illusion, goodness and negativity, are forces on a see-saw. The more we destroy illusion and negativity, the more we can appreciate and reveal spirituality and truth.

The Talmud addresses this by saying, "If someone says that Rome and Jerusalem are both built, or that Rome and Jerusalem are both destroyed, don't believe him. But if he says that Rome is in ruins and Jerusalem is built, or that Rome is built and Jerusalem is in ruins, believe him."[8] This means that goodness is concealed to the degree that evil is rampant, and that evil is destroyed to the degree that goodness is revealed. In other words, when people do negative things, defined as going against God's will, they camouflage goodness. But when we destroy negativity by following God's will, it makes it that much easier to recognize and appreciate goodness.

The Romans brought us to our present (and final) exile when they destroyed the Second Temple more than 1,900 years ago. They personified the opposite of Jerusalem's goodness because they were so steeped in all kinds of immorality, including self-serving hedonism, brutality, and idolatry. Since good and evil are opposites, only one of these forces and ideologies can be at its peak at any given time. If the hedonism and immorality of Rome is at its peak, we can't see goodness. If Jerusalem's godly and moral way of life is strong, it obscures what Rome represents. Both evil and good cannot vacate the world at the same time. To the extent that one is present, the other must be absent.

The more we obey God, the more we reveal His presence. Every time we make the effort to stop doing the wrong things we uncover something positive that was waiting to be revealed. We don't have to be total saints in order to feel our Creator's closeness and goodness. Every step that we take in the right direction gets rewarded.

A major theme in Judaism is that good automatically emerges as we remove the "dirt" of our misdeeds. We each have a tremendous well of inner goodness that we obscure whenever we stray from our soul's mission. Whenever we reject unholy temptations, our true essence, which is good, shines forth.

## Free Will

The Torah requires us to observe 613 commandments. Approximately 270 of these commandments can be done today. Gentiles are required to observe seven Noachide principles, encompassing sixty to seventy of these laws. Yet only a minority of Jews and Gentiles observe the laws that apply to them. Why is it that people disobey God so freely?

The answer is that He doesn't punish us, or reveal Himself to us, in obvious ways because that would take away our free will.[9] If we constantly saw or felt God's nearness, or if

He immediately punished us for our wrongdoings, we would never be tempted to do the wrong things, and we would do the right things by default. That would defeat the whole purpose of our being here. We are supposed to choose to be moral, not act properly only as a matter of self-preservation or robotic behavior. Even though evil's existence seems to contradict the idea that God is totally good, He saw fit to make it an integral part of His grand plan for the world. That plan lets us achieve greater reward by being tempted to act negatively, then rejecting ungodly choices.

God's giving us free will results in some people doing bad things. We wonder why God lets such people prosper and why some of them never seem to pay a price for their misdeeds. When we see a lot of apparently senseless suffering,[10] we may not recognize it as resulting from the divine gift of free will that was meant to ultimately benefit us. Instead, we may wonder if God has lost interest in running the world, or is not all-powerful and all-good as Judaism says He is.

God wants us to make choices that express His will for us. But when we don't, He hopes that we will learn from our mistakes. Experience is our best teacher. We can only learn how bad certain things are if He lets us do them. Were He to prevent us from disobeying Him, we might think that violating His will was harmless.

Instead, He gives us opportunities to experience the emptiness and disillusionment that come from thinking that we know better than He does what is best for us. When that happens, we are stricken by the sobering feeling that we have lowered and sullied ourselves, and feel hollow inside because we have estranged ourselves from God. When those feelings strike, we get a taste of what violating His will has done. Hopefully, that motivates us to search our souls and improve our behavior, to reinstate our intimacy with God and identify with our spiritual greatness and soul's potential.

Besides giving us free will, evil exists so that we will appreciate the Almighty's power when He finally metes out justice. Since it is no feat to overpower a weak force, He lets negativity become extremely powerful, then vanquishes it to show that He is the only Power. As long as evil seems to be everywhere, some people think that there is no God. By letting evil function when He wishes, then overcoming it when He wants it to stop, He let us appreciate that He is totally in control of the world.

Religions and nations have conceptualized negativity as an independent force or personified it as demons, Satan, or evil beings. The Zoroastrians even worshiped one god who controlled good and a different god who controlled evil. This contradicts the idea that God is One. His Oneness implies that no power, including evil, has any force unless He desires it to be so.

When we see evil all around us, it is hard to believe that it is part of a divine plan. The Shema reminds us that what the Torah teaches us about God and life is more real and meaningful than what we see and experience. He wants only to be good to us, and He lets evil and suffering predominate as part of a magnificent plan that will ultimately contribute to the world's spiritual rectification. Although we may not *feel* or experience that now, in the Messianic era we will do both. Then, the world will be totally rectified, and we will *see* how letting wicked people have their way was part of God's ultimate goodness.

God did not intend evil to exist eternally. He only put it here so that we would be challenged by it, see that it lacks true substance, and reject it. Doing this lets us internalize true goodness instead of it being an abstract idea. Once evil fully serves its intended purpose, it will be totally eradicated forever.

## God's Oneness

We say in the Shema that God is One, meaning that He is singular, unique, and incomparable. His uniqueness includes the idea that all else exists and functions only according to His will. He, of course, exists and functions without depending on anything else.

The idea of God's singularity encompasses the first three of Maimonides' Thirteen Principles of Faith:

1. *I believe with complete faith that the Creator, blessed is His Name, creates and guides all creations, and He alone made, makes and will make all things.*

This principle states that God has no "assistants" nor partners when He runs the world. This contrasts with pagan beliefs that many forces run the world and Christian beliefs that God is part of a trinity. This principle also includes the idea that the world only exists because of God's constant will for it to be sustained.

2. *I believe with complete faith that the Creator, blessed is His Name, is unique, that there is no uniqueness like His in any way, and that He alone is our God who was, is, and always will be.*

God cannot be divided into component parts because He is a total unity that is indivisible.

3. *I believe, with complete faith, that the Creator, blessed is His*

*Name, has no body and is not affected by physical events, and He has absolutely no physical likeness.*

The idea of God's unity reminds us that our world's many creations do not function and exist independently. They all operate under God's providence.[11] One of the Shema's main functions is to underscore this unity.

During Creation, the world expanded to the extent that God exclaimed, "If I create one more physical thing, the world will conceal Me so much that people won't be able to find Me. Enough concealment!"[12] God wanted our world to operate via natural laws of cause and effect that would conceal His "directing the show" behind the scenes. At the same time, He wanted people to find Him. Some concealment was necessary to challenge us to use our free will to find and obey God. But He wanted us to grow from the challenges of the physical world, not assume that natural forces are in charge and that He is absent. Believing that the physical world is ultimate reality, and ignoring God's presence and will, negates the world's entire purpose.

The Almighty hides within the physical world and wants us to look for Him there. All life and blessing filters down here through Him, although we sometimes believe that other forces, such as nature, luck, fate, or people, ultimately make things happen. The more we believe that He is the only force that rules us, the less energy we waste compromising ourselves and trying to placate and control other forces. For example, if we believe that our efforts alone control our financial destiny and security, we might lie, act unethically, or compromise ourselves trying to get whatever financial benefits we can. If we believe that doctors restore our health, we look to them alone when we are sick and leave God out of the picture. If we think that we are fully responsible for our achievements, we try to accomplish goals on our own without asking for God's help.

The blessings that we receive actually depend upon how connected we are to our Source. The more we bond with and rely only upon Him, the more blessing we receive, and the less secondary forces distract us. Since "a servant can only serve one master," tying ourselves to extraneous forces makes us less available for a relationship with the Almighty. While He wants us to do our utmost to take care of our health, earn a living, and get what we need within the constraints of the physical world, we need always remember that God is the only *ultimate* Source. Finding a balance between having faith in Him while doing what we must to live in a material world is an ongoing, lifelong challenge.

When we get distracted by this world's superficiality, we think that it is ultimate reality. That prevents us from noticing the divine Presence behind the scenes. The more He seems absent, the more people tend to do negative things that fill the apparent void. That only makes Him even more hidden.

We can only see and appreciate God's unity and unique-ness by constantly searching for it. That is why the Hebrew word for "world" is *olam*. It derives from the word *he'elem*, meaning "concealed." God designed a world that conceals His presence so that we can be rewarded for looking for Him. Searching for and finding Him lets us discover a hidden world of spiritual treasures that we aren't aware of otherwise.

## Serving God

Rabbi Moshe Chaim Luzzatto said that the Almighty set up the world in a way that we enjoy blessing and comfort, and have a tremendous sense of peace and security, when we acknowledge and willingly serve Him. On the other hand, we lose all goodness, and darkness and evil prevail, if we rebel against His rule.[13]

We fuel the existence and power of evil by not seeing God's unity. Therefore, the more He reveals, and we acknowledge, His unity, the more we destroy evil. The entire world's rectification depends upon this.[14]

Since God gave us the Torah, we know that He runs the world, and we are supposed to be witnesses who testify to that fact.[15] Even though the Torah tells us how to live and what to believe, we still struggle not to do the wrong things. We are conflicted because we aren't sure that God, and what He wants for us, are real. We may believe it intellectually, but not feel it emotionally. Our emotions tell us to gratify our physical drives and egos, and we  often rationalize doing unholy acts. The less real God seems, intellectually and emotionally, the harder it is for us to fight our material, egocentric and sensual drives. We can only devote ourselves totally to what we think is real, and worldly pleasures and distractions often feel more real to us than spirituality and God.

All of creation has but one Cause and purpose, but the roundabout and complex ways by which the Almighty runs the world make it hard to see that.[16] In the future, His reality and unity will be revealed to one and all, as the prophet Zechariah said, "In that day God will be one, and His Name will be one."[17]

God's uniqueness is only apparent if we see goodness and negativity as part of a divine plan where human actions and evildoing only succeed as much as He allows them. We write many of history's chapters, but He responds to our actions in ways that will lead to His ending. At the end of days, His revelation of the play's final act will show His total goodness throughout.

Each scene must first play out before God can show His total goodness. When we finally see the entirety of world history, we will know that He was sitting in the Director's chair all along. We will marvel at how He continually made sure that the world's purposeful end was achieved in the shortest, and best, possible way, while allowing us to exercise our free will.

### Notes

1. See Maimonides' Second Principle of Faith.

2. Genesis 1:3.

3. Ibid. 1:6-7.

4. Ibid. 1:14.

5. Rabbi Moshe Chaim Luzzatto, *The Way of God* 1:3:1.

6. Ibid.

7. Ibid. 1:5:8 and 4:4:1.

8. *Megillah* 6a.

9. When we violate God's will, we often suffer from punishing consequences that are inherent in the behavior itself. For example, if we act immorally, other people may want little to do with us. Our poor choices can erode our self-esteem, or make us so committed to the wrong path that we are too embarrassed to act morally. Although we can always repent, sometimes it is much easier to repeat our misdeeds, or not learn from our mistakes.

10. Our choices cause much of the world's misery. It is men who

often bring war upon themselves; famine and illness, too, are often caused by man's greed or poor life choices. Some suffering also results from God's punishing us in this world for our inappropriate actions. He does this to help us rectify the spiritual damage that we caused, reinstate closeness with Him, and educate us about how to act better.

11. *The Way of God* 4:4:1.

12. Ibid. 4:4:3. The divine name "*Sha-dai*" comes from the phrase, "He said to His world, 'enough' (***she'****amar le'olamo* ***dai***)."

13. Ibid. 4:4:3.

14. Ibid. 4:4:1.

15. Isaiah 43:12.

16. *The Way of God* 4:4:1.

17. Zechariah 14:9.

# 2

# Historical Background
# of the Shema

The Midrash (homiletical explanation of the Torah) gives two historical sources for the first two verses of the Shema prayer: "Hear, Israel, the Lord is our God, the Lord is One," and "Blessed is the Name of His glorious kingdom forever and ever."

One midrash[1] describes our forefather Jacob being on his deathbed, surrounded by his children. He prophetically saw his descendants suffering so terribly that they questioned God's ways. He wanted to ensure that they would withstand the challenges and tribulations of exile while retaining their faith, by revealing to his sons the events that would lead to the coming of the Messiah. He was not going to tell them when the Messiah would arrive, nor could he, because the Jews' behavior will determine when the Messiah arrives. Rather, Jacob wanted to tell his children how the darkest times in their history would contribute to a good end. Unfortunately, he lost his prophetic vision and divine inspiration a moment before he could do this.

Jacob wondered if his children's blemished faith had caused God to prevent him from revealing how Jewish suffering would eventually lead to future goodness. If so, his sons must have unresolved theological questions that Jacob could help put to rest. Since his children were going to be the pillars of the Jewish nation, if they thought that God was unfair or unjust, how would their descendants fare millennia later? The latter would be so far removed from people like Jacob that their doubts would topple them spiritually.

This prompted Jacob to ask his sons, "Do you have any complaints about God?"

His children unanimously responded, "Hear, Israel (one of Jacob's names), the Lord (who is compassionate) is our God (who metes out justice), the (compassionate) Lord is One." Thus, they stated their belief that one loving God executes justice and runs the world.

Jacob was ecstatic when he heard their response. It reassured him that he would leave behind twelve sons who had perfect faith in God and who would be a strong foundation for the Jewish nation. He joyfully responded, "Blessed is the Name of His glorious kingdom forever and ever."

This midrash says that the Jewish people subsequently got the mitzvah of saying the Shema in the merit of Jacob's sons' response. The tribes' strong faith was also indelibly etched into the spiritual persona (collective unconscious) of the Jewish people forever. Our ancestors enabled every one of their descendants to believe that everything ultimately has a good purpose.

Throughout history, Jews suffered torture and martyrdom while declaring their faith in God as they said the Shema. For example, Rabbi Akiva died with the Shema on his lips as he bled from wounds inflicted by the Romans. During the Crusades and the Inquisition, Christians tortured and martyred hundreds of thousands of Jews who refused to renounce their religion and who expired while saying the Shema. The same happened when countless Jews were murdered by Nazis and Nazi sympathizers. This type of Jewish fortitude was possible because Jacob's children said the Shema around his deathbed.

A second midrashic explanation traces the Shema's roots to the giving of the Ten Commandments.[2] God told the Israelites the First Commandment, "I am the Lord your God who brought you out of the land of Egypt, out of the house of slaves." They responded, "Hear, Israel." Then He uttered the Second Commandment, "You shall have no other gods before Me." The Jews replied, "The Lord is our God, the Lord is One." When the Almighty uttered each successive commandment, the Jews responded with corresponding verses from the Shema. In this way, the Shema formed part of the Jews' acceptance of the Ten Commandments. According to this midrash, the Israelites' response merited God's commanding them and their descendants to recite the Shema.[3]

These two midrashic explanations as to why we say the Shema apparently contradict each other. One says that we say the Shema because of Jacob's sons' faith, while the other attributes it to what the Israelites said when they received the Torah.

When two *midrashim* seem to contradict each other, it means that they are addressing different aspects of the same idea. One of the above *midrashim* refers to the aspect of the

Shema which Jacob and his children emphasized: our faith that God directs everything and, notwithstanding the pain and suffering that surrounds us, that we will ultimately realize His total goodness. We proclaim this faith when what we know — that God is totally good — and what we see and experience — that the world is full of pain and evil — are not congruent.

But the Shema has a second aspect to it. It expresses our Torah knowledge, which the Jews had when they received the Torah at Mount Sinai. When we accepted the Torah, we were simultaneously given the ability to understand its wisdom and absorb its deepest levels of truth. We can relate to God's uniqueness and unity because of the knowledge that Torah study gives, not because we have blind, non-rational belief.

## The Clarity of Torah

Torah is the best means for finding our inner selves. Its wisdom, truth, and energy can pierce the surface camouflages of God and let us discover what life is really about. Even if the rest of the world believe that their views of reality are true, Torah tells us that there is a spiritual system that is much more real than the purely physical world around us. Even when the physical world conceals God's singularity, our connection to Torah allows us to still see it.

When Jacob's sons surrounded his deathbed, they told him that they didn't understand God's ways, but believed in Him anyway. When the Jews received the Torah at Mount Sinai, they had clear knowledge and perceptions about God. They knew without a shadow of a doubt that He existed and was revealing absolute truth to them via the Torah. Their responding to each of the Ten Commandments with verses from the Shema meant that they saw God's unity through Torah. At that moment, they did not have to *believe* in God's unity — they *knew* it from their experience.

Throughout Jewish history, millions of Jews remained loyal to Judaism despite their lack of Jewish education because they inherited their faith from Jacob's children. Jews who are disconnected from Torah knowledge may still know the truth about God's existence and our obligation to be loyal to Him. When that happens, it is because they have blind faith, not because they understand the Almighty's ways.

Connecting to Torah gives us a certainty about how to live, despite what the rest of the world believes. A Jew who is strongly bound to Torah will survive the worst crises, while a Jew who is removed from Torah may or may not. Studying Torah always links us to what is happening behind the scenes and keeps us from despairing when we see only life's surface. This aspect of the Shema is rooted in the clarity and wisdom of Torah.

Because the Israelites in Egypt lacked this, they did not listen to Moses when he told them that they would soon go free. The Torah says that their "shortness of spirit and suffering from hard work" prevented them from believing him.[4] "Shortness of spirit" means that they were not connected to Torah. When that happens, Jews do not appreciate the reality that underlies the superficial world and can easily be overwhelmed by its difficulties and burdens.

When we pray the morning or evening services, we precede the Shema with a blessing about God's tremendous love for the Jews. We ask Him to inspire us and give us the wisdom to understand the Torah, to do what it asks of us, to understand its secrets, and to be excited by it.

Shortly after rising every morning, we are supposed to thank the Almighty for the privilege of being able to study Torah before we begin learning it that day. If we forget to say that blessing, we can fulfill our obligation to say it by reciting the prayer before the Shema asking God to help us learn Torah.

We precede the Shema by yearning to learn Torah because we can only truthfully say "Hear, Israel, the Lord is our God, the Lord is One" if we know Torah well. This verse expresses that we know God as clearly as the Israelites did at Mount Sinai. When the world around us seems full of injustice, and it is hard to believe that our lives are being guided by a divine Hand, only plumbing the depths of Torah and internalizing its message that God is running a purposeful world allows us to truly believe that He is One.

A midrash helps us understand how God can love and care for us when we feel that He has abandoned us.[5] It describes a king who married his fiancée after exchanging many love letters and promising to give her many gifts once they got married. Shortly after the wedding, though, she became promiscuous. Her disloyalty angered her husband and he abandoned her. Many months passed and people told the queen that her husband would never come back. They advised her to marry someone else. They were so persuasive that she almost followed their advice. She cried, thinking that they might be right, and sequestered herself in her chambers. She read his love letters, reviewed his promises, and reminisced about their wonderful times together. She finally concluded that her husband would inevitably return.

When her husband finally did come back after a very long time, the first thing he asked was, "How did you have the strength to wait for me for so many years?"

She responded, "I honestly don't know. But every time that I was ready to break down and give up hope, I took out all of your letters. I read about all of the things that we had shared, and something convinced me that deep, deep down, we still shared an enduring love."

And so it is with God and us. He wed the Jews, then we strayed from the way that we had agreed to live. We devoted ourselves to many pursuits besides God, so He eventually "left." The nations of the world came to us and said, "Your God left. He hasn't been around for years. You might as well forget about Him ever coming back. Come and join us. You'll prosper, have a good time, and be accepted by the world."

Our connection to Torah is the only thing that guarantees that our love relationship with God never ends, no matter what the illusions of life suggest. Throughout history, Jews reached their breaking point and were about to renounce their belief in, and commitment to, God. But by entering our house of learning and prayer and reading the Torah, something always convinced us that God would come back.

God will openly return to us when the Messiah comes. The first thing He will ask is, "How did you have the strength to wait for Me for so many years?"

We will respond, "Had we not revived ourselves by studying Torah whenever we verged on giving up, we would not have made it. Its messages convinced us of Your undying love for us."

## Summary

"Hear, Israel, the Lord is our God, the Lord is One" means that God runs the world, does everything for a good purpose, and has an unquenchable love for us. These ideas have been etched into our Jewish consciousness through Jacob and his descendants, as well as through the Torah. Historically, the Jew's tenacity of belief was often proportional to his or her connection to Torah. We could believe in God during national persecutions such as the Crusades, pogroms, and the Holocaust as long as we studied and internalized Torah. We cannot survive by divorcing ourselves from the Book of our covenant with the Almighty. If we do, we close the door that allows us to see that there is a God directing the play of history from start to finish.

### Notes

1. *Devarim Rabbah* 2:35.

2. Ibid. 2:36.

3. *Yerushalmi Berachot* 1:5 says that the Shema's verses allude to the Ten Commandments. It lists the corresponding verses as follows:

    Commandment #1: I am the Lord your God who brought you out of the land of Egypt, out of the house of bondage.

    It corresponds to: "Hear, Israel, the Lord is our God."

    Commandment #2: Don't have other gods before Me. This corresponds to: "...the Lord is One."

    Commandment #3: Don't take the Name of the Lord your God in vain. This corresponds to: "You should love the Lord your God."

    Commandment #4: Remember the Sabbath day to keep it holy. This corresponds to: "...so that you will remember and do all of My commandments." (Sabbath observance is compared to observance of the entire Torah.)

Commandment #5: Honor your father and your mother in order that your days be long upon the land that the Lord your God gives you. This corresponds to: "In order that your days...be many upon the land that the Lord swore to your forefathers to give them...."

Commandment #6: Don't murder. This corresponds to: "...and you will quickly be lost from the good land that the Lord gives you."

Commandment #7: Don't commit adultery. This corresponds to: "...don't stray after your hearts and after your eyes, that you lust after."

Commandment #8: Don't steal. This corresponds to: "...I will give the rain for your land in its proper time, the early rain and the late rains, and you will gather in your grain, your wine, and your oil." (This verse refers to your produce, not someone else's.)

Commandment #9: Don't bear false witness. This corresponds to: "I am the Lord your God in truth."

Commandment #10: Don't covet. This corresponds to: "...and write them on the doorposts of your house." (Not someone else's house.)

4. Exodus 6:9.

5. *Eichah Rabbah.*

# 3

## The Morning and Evening Shemas

We say the Shema every morning and evening because each Shema affects us, and the world, differently.

Performing any mitzvah changes the world because it draws spirituality here that wasn't here before. We make the world constantly change and grow this way. The daytime and evening Shemas each make a unique contribution to the world through this process.

God set up a purposeful world using Torah as His blueprint. He "hardwired" it with certain spiritual needs that only we can provide through our thoughts and actions. The specific times that we are supposed to do various mitzvot mesh with what the world, or we, need at those moments. The world was programmed to respond to our actions such that serving God brings blessing and fulfillment, while shirking our spiritual responsibilities brings evil and destruction.

When we say the Shema, we proclaim our belief that God is One and unique. We also proclaim that He is our King. (This is implied in the word "*Elokeinu*.") Since a king requires subjects, we must have a relationship with our Ruler where we agree to serve Him. Accepting this relationship automatically opens up spiritual channels for us. He responds to our desire to connect to Him by deepening His connection to us.

We determine the depth of our mutual closeness. Every time that we say the Shema, we construct spiritual bridges between our Creator and His world. Any time that we erect barriers by violating His will, we shut down the flow from His wellsprings of blessing.

Just as light pushes away darkness, doing mitzvot clears away spiritual darkness by drawing God's radiance here. Every time that we say the Shema, we make the entire world a better place. Each connection that we build between God and His world brings more spiritual light here.

We sin when, at least momentarily, we don't believe that following God's Torah is really what's best for us. Whenever we feel that way, we haven't internalized the Shema's message that God is unique and completely committed to a loving relationship with us. We can only fully open ourselves up to receiving His love by following the Torah.

When even one Jew properly says the Shema, he or she draws down a level of credibility about God's unity and Kingship that spills over to others. The more people say the Shema, the more real His presence, immanence, and omnipotence become.

When the world changes fundamentally, such as when night turns to day or when day turns to night, we are supposed to say the Shema. At these times, we state that God made a purposeful world and constantly watches over it. As the nature of the day or night changes, we can see God's wisdom in recognizing that we need both day and night.

The fact that the world constantly changes, yet has an orderliness to it, shows that the world has a Leader and a purpose.

Thus, the world is, and has always been, full of God. It will continue to be that way until the end of time. The world constantly functions according to His will and eventually will reach the goals that He intended for it since the time of Creation.

The Shema includes the ideas that God exists in the past, present, and future. He created the world and existed at the beginning of time; He is present now and shows Himself through the goings-on of the world; and He will also be here in the future and will guarantee that the world's spiritual purpose will come to fruition.

The morning Shema gives a different message than does the evening one. This is because God determined that the world should function differently during the day than at night. The spiritual laws that uniquely govern each period return and reassert themselves every morning and evening. These patterns of spiritual functioning are known as the "order of the day" and the "order of the night."[1]

We can best understand these differences by knowing something about the morning and evening prayers. The morning prayer, *Shacharit*, addresses the order of the day, and the evening prayer, *Maariv*, addresses the order of the night.

## The Patriarchs' Prayers

Our patriarch, Abraham, initiated the concept of saying morning prayers. Isaac did the same for the afternoon prayers, and Jacob did likewise for the evening services. This does not mean that there were Jewish prayerbooks in biblical times. Rather, our forefathers instituted the idea of communicating with God at specific times each day.

Several hundred years after our patriarchs died, God commanded the Jews to offer sacrifices in the morning and afternoon. Some of these sacrifices continued to burn on the altar all night. The sacrifices ceased before the Second Temple was destroyed more than 1900 years ago, but the specific prayers that once accompanied them are still said. These prayers were, and are, offered at the times of the morning and afternoon sacrifices, and also correspond to the times that our forefathers prayed.

Our respective forefathers did not simply compose prayers in the order in which they lived. Since the Jewish day starts at night, we might have expected Abraham, the first patriarch, to have composed the evening prayer. But this was not the case, because the order in which the patriarchs composed the daily prayers was based on factors other than chronology.

Each patriarch represented a specific attribute. Abraham discovered God by noticing the Almighty's lovingkindness, and Abraham was exceptionally kind himself. Being so kind, he was fully aware of how much God gives to us. Someone who is selfish finds it hard to imagine that others give selflessly. Since Abraham was a selfless person, he recognized kindness in others, and in God. The more he recognized His Creator's giving, the more he tried to emulate God by giving even more to others.

By contrast, Isaac represented self-discipline, character modification, and self-control. Jacob exemplified a combination of his father Isaac's and grandfather Abraham's attributes. He perfectly balanced lovingkindness (*chessed*) with discipline (*gevurah*), thereby expressing the attribute of truth and beauty (*emmet*).

We can imagine Abraham's excitement when he arose every morning and thought about the many opportunities to do loving acts that day. This helped him experience God most intensely at the start of every day. The morning prayer that he initiated extols God's lovingkindness in giving us another day.

The Shema incorporates this concept insofar as it declares that everything that happens during the day depends upon God's will and leads towards a goal. He doesn't let the world run willy-nilly. Instead, He takes care of and nurtures His world at every moment. The morning Shema expresses the fact that He is a Creator, a Nurturer, and a Controller of the world's direction. We reinforce these ideas at the start of every day to give us a proper perspective about how to live and make full use of the day's opportunities. With the start of each day, we sense His lovingkindness by reminding ourselves that everything comes from Him and moves towards His goals.

God's giving would be meaningless if it had no direction or purpose. His greatest kindness is in giving to us while allowing us to have free will, yet insuring that the world will reach His goal for it. He does this by supervising the world behind the scenes and directing it meaningfully moment by moment.

We say the afternoon prayer, *Minchah*, between mid-day and sunset. This necessarily interrupts our day. We may be working or taking care of important matters, yet we must suddenly take a break in order to pray. This requires discipline. It also reminds us not to get so caught up in our daily pursuits that we neglect God's values. It is difficult to act corruptly in business, or to harm God's other children, if we know that we will pray the afternoon  service minutes later. If we sincerely pray *Minchah* instead of merely giving it lip service, it is difficult to misbehave for the rest of the day.

Just as we schedule meetings with important people throughout the day, we schedule daily appointments with God. When we have daily meetings with the One Above, we won't want our other appointments to violate the tenor of that encounter.

Since Isaac was a man of discipline *par excellence*, he understood that the middle of the day is the most critical time for discipline. He composed the afternoon prayers, which are considered the prayers of self-discipline, because they interrupt the day and help us stay on a moral track.

Jacob suffered a great deal during his lifetime and underwent trials and tribulations that were a portent of what would happen to the Jews in exile. His hallmark was truth, and he showed his descendants how to have faith in God during the darkest times of Jewish history, when the Almighty's Presence and giving would seem hidden. Jacob initiated the evening prayer, *Maariv*. At night, God holds back from giving. He shows His giving most during daylight hours since that is a time of action. People work and accomplish things primarily when it is light outside. When darkness descends, they begin the process of winding down and preparing to sleep.

Since nighttime is characterized by God's holding back, unholy forces have an easier time taking over the world then. People are more likely to sin at night, not only because we are busier during the day and have less time to do the wrong things, but because the night's spiritual atmosphere is deficient in God's energy.

This is why the nighttime Shema has two aspects: 1. It reminds us that night is created by God just as day is. 2. It reinforces that God's holding back will eventually have positive effects. We say the Shema at night when we see God's withholding. That helps us confront darkness with a sense of faith and belief.

Jacob was able to reconcile God's lovingkindness with His withholding and saw no inconsistency between the two. The balanced compromise between kindness and discipline is truth and belief. When things don't seem to go well for us, we need to keep believing that God and Judaism are truthful and meaningful. Since Jacob's hallmark was truth, he composed the evening prayer that reminds us of that.

This is why Jacob was considered the father of the Diaspora. He had four major crises, each of which prepared us for the respective exiles that we would undergo. His ability to discern truth blazed the path of survival for his descendants in exile. Since truth is not apparent in the darkness of exile, surviving the Diaspora required Jacob's attribute.

When we are in exile, we wonder if God loves us, and if He is truly giving. Sometimes, such as during the Inquisition, pogroms, or the Holocaust, we have felt that He is only withholding and punitive. We needed someone with a balanced sense of kindness and discipline — i.e., truth — to decipher the enigmas of exile. Only such a person could be a model of how to believe in God despite the apparent contradictions that constantly confront us.

This is why we follow the evening Shema by saying, "I am

the Lord your God, *emmet ve'emunah* (truth and belief)." By contrast, in the morning we say, "I am the Lord your God, *emmet ve'yatziv* (it is true and firm)." This latter verse means that the God of lovingkindness is also the God of discipline, and we see that it is true. In the evening, we say that the God of discipline is also loving and kind; however, we can't *see* this truth at night. We merely *believe* it. This idea was best conveyed by Jacob, which is why he composed the evening prayer.

Some of our greatest challenges to belief in God have come during the night of Jewish history.[2] This is why we acknowledge His lovingkindness in the morning by saying the Shema, then repeat it at day's end when we no longer see His love and wonder where He is. The morning Shema is a statement of recognition; the evening Shema is one of belief. Despite the darkness in which we are immersed, we believe that it came from God and that He is nurturing us through it and leading us in a meaningful direction.

The daytime Shema recognizes that God was, is, and always will be a loving and kind deity. The order of the night requires us to declare that we believe He is loving and kind even when we no longer see it.

Maimonides said that a prime time to learn Torah is at night, when everything goes to sleep and all of the day's distractions disappear. According to him, the "crown of Torah" can only be earned by someone who learns Torah at night.

From sunset until midnight, our Creator's show of kindness dwindles. After midnight, we enter the dawning of the next day's divine kindness and giving. This is why midnight was designated as a special time to pray for the rebuilding of the Temple. Since God's lovingkindness starts building as night ebbs away and day is in the offing, we ask Him to take away the spiritual night (destruction and exile) and bring on the day (redemption). As we notice the physical world's transition from darkness to light, we ask God to activate the spiritual world, dispel our spiritual darkness, and bring on the dawn of the Messiah.

This is why some people learn Torah at night. They sleep while it is still day and wake up at midnight to recite psalms and pray for the rebuilding of the Temple and Jerusalem. Then they learn Torah until daybreak and pray the morning service as the sun rises. This capitalizes on the fact that time moves towards day after midnight. As the night goes on, a momentum builds towards God's manifestation of kindness in the morning.

In a beautiful metaphor, the Talmud says that God, as it were, cries at night over the Temple's destruction. That God "cries" means that He holds back from giving when He really wants to give. As midnight passes, He "feels" a sense of loss over the Temple's destruction. This is a time when we capitalize on our Heavenly Father's "weeping" and cry over the Temple's destruction ourselves. This promotes the rebuilding of the Temple.

This is but one example of how thorough the structure of our service to God was meant to be. Authentic prayer is intimately connected to our daily lives. The way we worship, as well as when we do mitzvot, has a unique connection to the period of time in which our actions occur.

## Hidden Reasons

All Jewish rituals and prayer services were well planned and have apparent and obvious rationales, as well as hidden ones. The hidden reasons are known only to those who are versed in the Torah's secrets.

The following illustrates one such "secret":

There are two ways to grow spiritually: We can sense our shortcomings by comparing ourselves to God's awesomeness and perfection, then yearn to approach His greatness. This type of humility can motivate us to improve and relate to our Creator in a more authentic way.

A second path toward spiritual growth is to feel God's embrace. This comes from opening ourselves up to God's love and concern, not from assessing our shortcomings and sensing the need to improve. Our desire to be close to Him motivates us to be better so that we can be worthy of receiving and reciprocating His love.

On week days, our spiritual growth comes from relating to the King of kings with an honest, yet sometimes unhappy perspective about ourselves. The Sabbath, though, is a holy time when we shouldn't feel depressed or sad. We are supposed to use its elevated spirit and sanctity to feel joyful and enthused, and engage those feelings as a steppingstone for approaching God. It is neither a day for introspection nor for utter humility.

When the Temple stood, Jews became spiritually blocked ("ritually impure") when they touched a corpse.[3] Ritually impure Jews could not enter the Temple until they were sprinkled with a solution containing a red heifer's ashes. This sprinkling removed their spiritual blockage and could be done any day of the week except for the Sabbath. Ostensibly, this was because a person who was desperate to regain ritual purity might violate the Sabbath by carrying the ashes from one domain to another, a constructive activity that is forbidden on the Sabbath.

This is the "obvious" reason that sprinkling ashes on the Sabbath was forbidden. The "hidden" reason, though, was because sprinkling ashes on people made them feel humble, which was at odds with the spirit of the Sabbath. Jews are supposed to feel happy, not lowly, on the Sabbath.[4]

This is but one example of how well thought-out all Jewish rituals and prayers are. None is haphazard or random. All Jewish worship is designed to be integrated with the spiritual energy of the time-frame in which it occurs. That is why we serve God one way during the week and a different way on the Sabbath. There is a symphony between us, God, and the universe, and these interactions differ on the Sabbath and weekdays. If we want to grow spiritually, we must use the universe's spiritual chemistry with us one way during the week and another way on the Sabbath.

The two Shemas reflect this idea. The morning Shema expresses our exhilaration at experiencing God's love for us. We affirm that He created, nurtures, and directs the world. But we express different sentiments in the evening Shema. We individually confront darkness at night, while Jews as a nation confront exile. At these times, we take it on faith that God created, nurtures, and directs the world. The words of both Shemas are identical, but the heart and soul that go into each are unique to the orders of the day and night.

How rich and beautiful is the Jewish service of God! It incorporates the ideas that the day is a time of goodness and lovingkindness, while at night we struggle to see that. Each Shema expresses a different nuance of our relationship with the Almighty and His conduct with the world.

When we say the Shema every morning in appreciation of His lovingkindness, we build a bridge that guarantees that our Creator will keep on giving. At night, we declare our belief that God runs and will always run the universe. That guarantees that He will turn night into day. In this way, the evening Shema becomes a beacon in the midst of our darkness.

## Notes

1. The daily orders change, but God's existence stays constant and invariable, absolute and independent of anything else.

2. Our other great challenge comes when we live with success and affluence and don't appreciate the fact that God, not we, brought us our gifts as loans to use properly.

3. Contact with a corpse still makes Jews ritually impure, but everyone today is assumed to be in that state since we don't currently have the means for removing it. Since ritually impure people are forbidden to enter the Temple Mount in Jerusalem, Jews today may not go there. Even though the Temple was destroyed, the land on which it stood retains its holiness.

4. See *Shem MiShmuel.*

# 4

## Hear, Israel...

Having discussed general ideas underlying the Shema, it is easier to appreciate the meaning of its words.

The first verse of the Shema means, "Listen, Jewish people, the Lord is our God, the Lord is One." God has seventy-two Hebrew names, each of which refers to a different way that He manifests Himself to us. While we can't really understand His essence, describing His conduct with us gives us a way to relate to Him.

We should try to get to know all of God's facets, not only those that are emotionally appealing to us, such as His obvious kindness and love.

The name "Lord" in the Shema's first verse, *yod-keh-vav-keh* (*YKVK*) in Hebrew, refers to the Almighty when He manifests His compassion. "Our God" (*Elokeinu*) refers to Him when He acts as a Ruler who metes out justice. The third mention of God in this verse, "the Lord is One," is again *YKVK*. This three-fold repetition means that God is one and the same loving deity, whether He reveals Himself to us as a God of compassion or as a God of justice. Everything He does stems from His love for us, although He must sometimes act harshly with us in order to effect justice.

Since Abraham's time, we have been challenged to see God as One regardless of how He deals with us. Abraham's relationship with God was built on lovingkindness, so the Almighty tested him with ten trials that were geared towards teaching him that the Master of the World also acts with discipline and justice.

During one of these trials, God told Abraham that He planned to destroy Sodom and its neighboring four cities.[1] Being a compassionate man, Abraham prayed for an entire day that the One Above would spare them. First he asked that the cities be spared if there were fifty righteous people living there. When God agreed, Abraham lowered the number to forty-five. The Lord agreed again, so Abraham continued bargaining about the number of righteous people whose merit would allow the wicked inhabitants to be spared. Finally, he reached the smallest reasonable number whose presence would be reason to withhold the destruction. When the All-Merciful One agreed that He would spare the cities if a mere ten righteous people lived there, Abraham understood that the cities were doomed. They lacked even a minimal number of decent people. God, in His mercy, then sent an angel to rescue Abraham's nephew Lot and Lot's family from the impending calamity.

Abraham prayed continually from a vantage point overlooking all five cities that they would be saved. Viewing people who were slated for destruction moved him to pray with every fiber in his body. But his prayers were not answered as he hoped, and God annihilated the cities' inhabitants by day's end.

The very next morning, Abraham stood in exactly the

same place that he had prayed for the people's salvation the day before. Even though he now saw five decimated cities, he still "rose early in the morning" and prayed.[2]

It might seem strange that he prayed at the very same spot where his prayers were not answered the day before. This incident teaches us that God's need to destroy irredeemably wicked people does not contradict His love for His world. Abraham understood that God's love sometimes requires meting out justice, and he accepted God even when He didn't do what Abraham wanted. During his lifetime, Abraham became spiritually great as he learned to accept all of God's facets, the loving with the punitive, as he repeatedly saw the Almighty sometimes hold back from giving and sometimes punishing.

We express this idea in the Shema when we say that the Lord of compassion and the God of justice are one and the same. We can become spiritually great, as Abraham did, by accepting a relationship with all of God's facets, not only with the ones that make us comfortable.

## Our God

We say in the first verse of the Shema that the Lord is "our God."[3] This is because the entire world does not yet accept God as we know Him, nor do most Gentiles follow the seven Noahide Principles of morality. Since Jews have historically believed in one true God, and we accepted His Torah, we can honestly say that He is "our God."[4]

The fact that God exists does not make Him "our God." He is only our God if we have a relationship with Him where we do what He requires of us.

God does not exist only for us, even though the rest of

the world does not yet accept Him as we do. He will eventually be a God for all peoples just as He is for us now. That is why the Shema says that He is "our God," followed by, "the Lord is One." Ultimately, the entire world will serve only one God.[5]

Our deity's reality is so compelling that we proclaim with certainty that eventually He will be worshiped and recognized universally. We don't believe that our concept of the Almighty is good enough for us and that others can believe whatever they like. We look forward to the time when the entire world will accept the truth that we alone see today.[6]

## The "Witness" of the Shema

When we say, "Hear, Israel, the Lord is our God, the Lord is One," we are supposed to concentrate on the idea that He is everywhere (the "four corners of the earth and the seven heavens") and controls all worlds.

The last letter of the Hebrew word Shema (hear) is *ayin*. When the first verse of the Shema appears in the Torah, the *ayin* is written very large, as is the last letter of the verse, the *dalet* of the word *echad* (one). Together, these letters spell the word *ed*, meaning "witness." When these letters are reversed, they spell *da*, which means "know." This expresses the idea that Jews must be witnesses who know that God is One.

When we say the Shema, we accept the mission of bearing witness to a world that is not yet ready to accept Him that God exists. As His loyal subjects, we can't simply believe and accept that God is One, despite His many manifestations. We must bear witness to His unity by living a godly life that testifies to His existence.[7] We do this by living consistently as observant Jews who are not hypocritical. When observers see the difference between those who live godly lives and those who don't, our behavior testifies to the Almighty's existence.

A black army officer once had occasion to visit an observant Jewish accountant in Brooklyn. As they concluded their business, the students in the Orthodox girls' school across the street were leaving for the day. As the two men walked to the officer's car, he was so impressed by the girls' modest dress and behavior that he commented, "You can see God in those girls."

In King Solomon's time, people came from around the world to hear his wisdom and see how Jews lived. Jews at that time modeled to the world how godly people lived. When the Jews were under Roman rule, their beliefs and way of life were so impressive that 10 percent of the Roman empire became Jewish. In fact, the nephew of the Roman emperor Hadrian even converted to Judaism and became a renowned Torah commentator whose works Jews read to this day.

An American Christian minister once taught a marriage workshop for religious Christian couples. Toward the end of the course he told the participants, "Do you know who holds the secret to a happy marriage? The Jews do." He then proceeded to tell them about the Jewish laws of family holiness, and their wonderful spiritual and emotional effects.[8]

It is not enough for Jews simply to declare our faith and belief in principles. The lives we lead are the most compelling testimony to our true beliefs because our actions mirror God's reality to the world.

## "The Lord is our God-King"

Judaism teaches that God created us because He is all-good and all-giving and wanted to give us opportunities to merit His goodness. To this end, He made the world in a way that He seemingly needs us to desire His rule.

Although closeness to God feels wonderful, we term accepting His rule "receiving the yoke of Heaven." This is because no matter how wonderful any relationship is, at times we must do things for a partner that we really don't want to do. We do them because the relationship as a whole is good and meaningful, and we know that we must sometimes go against our nature to preserve it. Still, that kind of responsibility can feel like a yoke.

God's "Kingship" over us began when He gave us the Torah. He "courted" us when He took us out of Egypt, and we got to "know" Him during the next seven weeks. Our relationship reached its peak when we crowned Him King at Mount Sinai.

As was mentioned, God's essence is incomprehensible. He gave Himself names that reflect our understanding of His actions so that we would have a way of relating to Him. For example, when we call Him a Creator, we can better understand how He operates in our world. But besides being a Creator, He is also a King over all of creation. We strengthen His sovereignty when we accept Him as our King and obligate ourselves to serve Him. Just as a person needs people to rule in order to be a king, God's Kingship depends upon our desire to have a relationship with Him as our ruler.

His "Creatorship" never changes regardless of what we do. He exists no matter what we do and despite what happens to the world. We express this by saying that He is absolute and non-contingent. This is the aspect of God that we express by calling Him *Elokim*. When we call Him *Adon Kol* (the Master of All), we refer to the fact that He owns the entire world and rules it as He wishes. God expressed His desire to stay intimately involved with all that He created by designing a world where everything depends upon Him.

But besides being a God and Master of everything, He is also a King. In His infinite love for us, He lowered Himself into this world so that we could have a relationship with Him. Yet the quality of our mutual interaction depends upon our efforts to do mitzvot, refine our character traits, study Torah, and yearn to be worthy recipients of His giving. This is how the subjects' will grants the King His power.[9]

A dictator doesn't care if his subjects want him to rule or not. He forces them to obey him regardless of their desire. God could do that with us, yet He doesn't. He interacts with us only as much as we want to relate to Him. This is what we mean when we call God our King.

Even though the Almighty has no limitations, He lets us "strengthen" or "weaken" His rule over the world by determining the depth of our relationship with Him. The more we want Him to be close, and act accordingly, the more God lets us feel His Presence. The more we want Him out of the picture, the more He hides. Thus, God chose not to be a King when we don't want it. His exercise of power depends upon our loyalty to Him.

God chose not to be a dictator who makes unilateral decisions about how the world runs. Instead, He designed a system where we make choices and He responds to them. We can thereby "tie His hands" by avoiding Him and "force"

Him to withhold the blessing that He so much wants to give us. Biblical Hebrew describes two different kinds of rulers. A *shalit* or *moshel* rules without the people's ratification, while a *melech* rules with their willing obedience. The Almighty is a *moshel* over the nations of the world because He makes things happen to them whether or not they consent to it. By contrast, our commitment to Torah creates a unique relationship where God is our *melech* (King).

The first theme of the Shema is our proclamation of God's uniqueness. The second theme is our acknowledgement of Him as our ruler and our "accepting the yoke (government) of Heaven." We express this by calling Him "our God" (*Elokeinu*), and simultaneously noting our vital role as His loyal subjects.

The final verse of the last portion of the Shema says, "I am the Lord your God who brought you out of the land of Egypt to be your God. I am the Lord your God."[10] Rashi, a commentator on the Torah, says that even if we choose not to be His faithful subjects, the Lord is still our King, and He will force His rule upon us.

This creates a philosophical dilemma. If divine Kingship implies that we choose for Him to rule us, how can He force His rule upon us? Forced rule would make Him a dictator, not a King.

Rabbi Hutner, *zt"l*, explained that every Jew originally crowned God King when we received the Torah at Mount Sinai. We did this by saying, "*Na'aseh ve'nishma*" — "We will do whatever our King asks of us, then understand His rationale for giving us the commandments."[11] We show our loyalty to God's government by complying with the divine constitution (the Torah) that we ratified over 3,300 years ago.

The Jewish nation reached their spiritual peak when they

accepted the Torah, and they wanted always to retain that commitment to God. When they said, *"Na'aseh ve'nishma,"* they wanted Him to be their King forever. Meanwhile, they expected that they and their descendants would occasionally lose their commitment to God and Torah. Their proclamation, "We will do, then understand" included their hope that God would never abandon them nor "abdicate His Kingship" if their resolve ever weakened in the future.

Subjects don't only want a king to rule them when he is coronated. Their actions imply that they trust him implicitly and have no intentions of revoking his rule at a later time.

When the Jews crowned the Almighty as their King, they had unparalleled clarity of perception. They knew without a shadow of a doubt what was best for them. They couldn't retract their decision later by saying that they were confused when they made their initial statement of loyalty. They did not make a temporary decision for the Lord to be their King, with a proviso that they could change their minds in the future. They initially accepted God's Kingship with the assumption that it was irrevocable.

Even when Jews later rejected God as their King, He never let them go. He promised to take any means necessary to ensure that Jews would always let Him rule them. Although this may seem coercive, it actually ratified the original commitment that the Jews made when they were at their spiritual finest. (Before the Messianic era, God will again force the Jews to accept Him as King if we don't first do it ourselves.)

It is hard to appreciate the beauty of God being our King because we no longer live with the greatness of true royalty. Americans, in particular, don't like status differences, especially those of a king and his subjects. The idea that God is our King makes us think of fairy tales, or slavery, not lofty spiritual concepts. Also, corrupt, immoral, and inept leaders make us feel cynical about the nobility of royalty. We can hardly imagine wanting a King to rule us, yet it is essentially a very beautiful idea, whose essence we can incorporate into our lives.

## Summary

God's Kingship, as expressed in the Shema, began when we accepted the Torah. When the Jews heard the Ten Commandments, they responded with verses from the Shema that showed their commitment to doing, without reservation, whatever God would ask of them, forever. This was the way they accepted the "yoke of Heaven."

## Notes

1. Genesis 18:17–33; 19:27–28.

2. This is the verse from which the Talmud derived that Abraham authored the morning (*Shacharit*) prayer. It is also a source for the idea that we should have a fixed place to offer our daily prayers.

3. Deuteronomy 6:4.

4. Rashi on Deuteronomy 6:4.

5. *The Way of God* 4:4:1.

6. As in Zephaniah 3:9 and Zechariah 14:9.

7. This idea is expressed in Isaiah 43:12.

8. My thanks to Rabbi Joseph Friedman for sharing this story with me. It is interesting that the Gentile women thought that the

laws of family purity were a wonderful idea, but their spouses refused to go along with the restrictions!

9. These concepts are discussed in *The Way of God* 4:4:2.

10. Numbers 15:41.

11. Exodus 24:7.

# 5

# Perfecting the World

When we pray, we ask God for things, and hope that He will respond by giving them. We tend to think that He only hears us if He gives us what we ask for, but that is not true. He responds to every sincere prayer, although not necessarily in the way that we expected.

The purpose of prayer is not to tell God what we need so that He will know what to give us. He always knows exactly what we need. One reason we pray is because we can only receive the blessing that the Almighty wants to give by first connecting to Him.[1] The degree to which we bond to Him is the degree to which we can receive. We accomplish some of this bonding through prayer, where we initiate God's flow of blessing by building a bridge between us and Him.

God never has difficulty giving, but we are often not developed enough to properly receive from Him. In that respect, we may be unworthy of getting what we want. Prayer works not because we tell God what to give, but because we come closer to Him when we pray and make ourselves into better recipients of His blessing by changing. His greatest gift to us is the feeling of connection and closeness to Him that we get when we pray, not the material things that we ask for. Since every prayer connects us to God when we express our desire to merge with Him, communication through prayer never goes unrewarded.

Connecting to God takes away our feelings of isolation, and uniting with the Source of all goodness lets us feel the most intense pleasure possible. Once we connect to the Source, all goodness becomes available. Without connecting to Him, we have no authentic way of relating to His blessing.

If we sincerely tell the One Above, "I need a nicer home and a new car," we come closer to Him and make ourselves more ready to receive what He deems appropriate. That doesn't mean that we will necessarily get what we ask for, but we will definitely be rewarded with the consequences of building a bridge to the Master of the World.

If we finally get something after praying for it for a long time, it is not because we finally persuaded the Almighty to change His mind. It is because *we* changed by praying so much. We created an intense bond with Him that moved us to a higher spiritual level, which lets us receive gifts that we were not able to appreciate before.

We bond to God whenever we state in the Shema that He is our Creator and our King. That kind of bonding automatically makes the world a more blessed place because it draws God into an intimate relationship with us. Every divine involvement with this world must bring blessing because the world automatically becomes better the more it unites with its Creator. Saying the Shema creates this unity, which in turn causes more divine light to flow here.

Recognizing God's existence and kingdom brings blessing, while rebelling and rejecting the King's obligations cause darkness to descend and negativity to rule. God's degree of connection to the world determines how much blessing we enjoy, and His degree of disconnection determines how much we lose His blessing.[2]

God's blessing, as shown by His involvement with the world, creates good, light, peace, holiness, and purity that shatters the powers of negativity. Those harmful powers then become obligated to work for us instead of against us. Negativity cannot destroy goodness if the former is designated to serve people.

Once we connect God to His world, the forces of evil cannot ruin the good. Evil dies of malnutrition if it can't use goodness to serve it. This was included in the idea we discussed earlier that the stronger good is, the weaker negativity is, and vice versa.

Thus, a single Jew sitting alone can destroy negativity merely by saying the Shema. He or she creates a spark of light by connecting God to the world, which simultaneously dispels some of the darkness.

We constantly battle negativity on different levels every day. One level is through prayer and by bonding with the Almighty through saying the Shema.

When we don't accept the Almighty as our Ruler, we show that we don't want Him in our lives. He then "hides His face" because of our lack of interest. That conceals His power and lets negativity rule.

Negativity takes hold of the world to the extent that we push God out of it. When our actions tell the Almighty to stay away, negative forces fill the resulting vacuum.

The world desperately needs us to dispel its darkness! The more we strengthen ourselves by saying the Shema every day, the more we draw the divine Presence here, accept His rule, and affirm His centrality in our lives. The resulting on-slaught of powerful, positive forces automatically weakens the negative ones.

Divine blessing must come to the world every time we say the Shema, because the Shema links us to the Source of all blessing. When we say in the Shema that God is unique and One, we are also asking Him to reveal His unity and uniqueness. He responds by making both clearer to us and to all humanity. Our searching for and connecting to Him makes His unity and uniqueness more apparent. How much the world recognizes His kingdom depends upon our saying the Shema.

Rabbi Moshe Chaim Luzzatto wrote many prayers describing God's unity. After each one, he asked the Almighty to reveal His unity to the world. He did this because the degree to which we yearn for God to reveal Himself and bond with us is the degree to which He does both.

Every time that we say the Shema, we rectify the world a little more. Our daily actions cause the world's ultimate correction little by little. None of our spiritual efforts is ever lost. We construct some of the "building blocks" for the world's rectification by saying the Shema.

## We Bring Rectification

God deliberately created an imperfect world that can't rectify itself. We are the ones who make all of the world's spiritual corrections,[3] and allow divine light to flow here to dispel the darkness. We play an integral role in making it all happen because the Master of the World wanted us to perfect the world, then enjoy the fruits of our labor. He designed all things in the material world, and all events, with the potential to perfect the world, provided we use them properly.

When we make a better world, we deserve to experience its goodness. Our greatest sense of achievement and self-esteem comes from enjoying the results of our toil. If we played no role in correcting the world, or if it improved by itself, we couldn't totally relate to it, nor feel the full pleasure of enjoying a world that we built.

We are supposed to perfect the world by first spiritually fixing ourselves, yet some people try to improve the world by fixing only what is external to them. The world automatically gets rectified in ways that parallel how we fix our own spiritual flaws. We can't correct the world without first putting our own house in order.

For example, the more we see God's unity, the more the world can see it. The more we bond with our Heavenly Father, the more others will feel close to Him. Everything that occurs to us individually has a parallel effect on the world at large. Instead of looking for political causes to champion, we should first correct our own character defects and moral failings. That will have ripple effects on the world.

Ultimately, the world's perfection can only come from its Creator. Since only He is perfect, the extent to which we connect the world to Him determines how close to perfection it gets.[4] This makes our deeds very critical.

Our inner drives can push us to do positive or negative things. God expects us to develop the self-discipline to do what's positive and to suppress our drives to do what's negative. The more we act positively, the less time and energy we have to think and act harmfully.

Some people want to improve themselves but they aren't strong enough to control their negative inclinations. Rather than mustering all of their energy to constantly battle their negative drives, they usually achieve more by trying to do as much good as possible. That will automatically leave them with less time and energy to do what's wrong, and will inevitably weaken their negative urges.

Concentrating on doing what's right weakens negativity by default; it doesn't correct or transform it into something positive. Declaring God's unity and uniqueness in the Shema ties all forces to Him and testifies that negativity has no real force of its own. Since negativity comes from the Almighty, He can help us transform it into a force that is integrated with goodness.

We energize negativity by seeing it as an independent force and following its beck and call. By stating that all forces stem from our Creator's will, nothing can control or hurt us. Believing that God is One, and that all forces in the world are under His control, is our ultimate unification of Him. Stating that every day in the Shema corrects the world and brings it one step closer to truth and redemption.

## Summary

The Shema proclaims God as the world's Creator and Master. He stays intimately involved with His world all of the time because He is committed to its spiritual perfection through our efforts. When we say the Shema, we state our faith in these ideas, or acknowledge them based in our Torah learning.

We inherited the spiritual genes of Jacob and his sons, as well as those of our ancestors who received the Torah at

Mount Sinai. That makes us receptive to the belief that God always has been, and always will be, involved in our lives. Stating these beliefs in the Shema maintains a constant connection between our Creator and His world.

We are the critical links in a chain that draws the divine Presence here. The more we do this, the more people at large will feel the Almighty's Presence, too.

The morning Shema expresses our thanks to the Master of the World for giving us yet another day to appreciate His many acts of goodness. The nighttime Shema expresses our trust and belief in Him. Together they make our day full of His companionship.

### Notes

1. *The Way of God* 4:5:1.
2. Ibid. 4:4:3.
3. Ibid. 4:4:1 and 4:4:3.
4. Ibid. 1:2:3.

# 6

# How the Shema
# Encourages Spiritual Growth

Every day presents us with unique spiritual opportunities. In the secular world, Tuesday is qualitatively the same as Wednesday, and 9:00 today is qualitatively the same as 9:00 tomorrow. According to Judaism, however, time is not on a spiritual continuum. From a Jewish point of view, life has some continuity, but each day presents new gifts of spiritual potential that never existed before, and will never exist again. This means that once we lose a spiritual opportunity, it may be extraordinarily difficult to recapture, or may even be irretrievable. Each day's spiritual opportunity belongs to that day alone. We cannot simply make up for what we didn't achieve spiritually today by doing it tomorrow. Today has its unique opportunities, and tomorrow has its own. Every instant of our lives was intended to be used meaningfully.

The Torah expresses this by saying that our foremother Sarah lived one hundred years, and twenty years, and seven years.[1] Describing her lifespan this way teaches that she lived every day to the fullest.[2]

We often experience a discrepancy between the idea that we should live each day fully and actually making it happen. When we drag ourselves out of bed in the morning, we can wonder if we will have a meaningful day, or simply muddle through another twenty-four hours of struggle or boredom. We get the Monday morning blues confronting our secular responsibilities, and we get spiritual "Monday morning blues" every day. The latter happens when we must decide if we are willing to do God's work today and accept the yoke of His spiritual responsibilities, or take the day off from serving our Creator. Often, the best way to overcome such quandaries is to force ourselves to stop thinking and just get out of bed. Doing that puts us on the right track with a momentum that helps us do what we should.

Rabbi Luzzatto said that we go through the "blues" every morning because we must be challenged to become worthy of each day's new spiritual opportunity. The challenge itself is the door that opens up each day's potential.

Saying the Shema helps us fight the urge to hide from God every morning. It is the "energy cell" that recharges us and keeps us from succumbing to daily "spiritual blahs." It reminds us that life is only worthwhile if we live as authentic Jews with a critical spiritual role to fulfill every day. That pulls us out of our potential ruts.

The Shema reminds us every morning that life is only worth living if we infuse it with new meaning and constantly overcome new spiritual challenges. When we say the Shema, we should envision how beautiful a spiritually committed life is. That will encourage us to grab the day and go forward, instead of running away from the challenges ahead.

God's great wisdom determined that we should prepare

ourselves to sanctify our lives daily via the ultimate sacrifice.[3] Otherwise, we can easily squander our spiritual potential and mischannel our energies. God conveyed this idea by creating the world with the Hebrew letter *heh*.[4] A *heh* has two parallel vertical lines, with a horizontal line connecting them from above and an opening below. It resembles a house with a roof but no floor underneath. The opening below symbolizes that we will "fall out of the bottom" of the world if we only exist physically without developing our spiritual potentials. We develop ourselves by accepting challenges and responsibilities.[5] The *heh* reminds us how tempted we are to abandon our moral dedication and live easy lives with little meaning. Since God knows our weaknesses, He gave us commandments to nurture our moral strength and resist inappropriate temptations.

Our world is not inherently holy, although we can invest it full of sanctity. When we accept spiritual challenges, we run the risk of succumbing to negativity. But if we meet the challenges and add to the world's holiness and spiritual beauty, we elevate it. We then get rewarded by enjoying the holiness that we brought here.

When God left the world spiritually incomplete, He wanted all of the world's people to spiritually perfect it over many generations, in different ways, through diverse experiences. We can only rectify the world by pushing past our basic inertia and emotional resistances and working hard to push away the darkness.

Every time we do God's will, we add a spiritual dimension to the world. Having proper intentions while saying the Shema is a wonderful way to bring spiritual brilliance into the world.[6] One introspective thought of total dedication to

God can bring an awesome and powerful rectification to the world.

By definition, spiritual growth must challenge us, and we can't grow without a struggle. Our purpose in life is to overcome spiritual challenges, not live lives of comfort and pleasure. When life is difficult, we may feel defeated or alone, yet we are not. No Jew ever has to draw God "down from heaven" by himself or herself. Our efforts are always part of the collective efforts of the entire Jewish people. If we say the morning Shema believing that life is worthless without Judaism, we enable the rest of the world, even people whom we don't know, to reach great spiritual heights! Our proper intentions while saying the Shema make it easier for any searching Jew to feel God's closeness. Without that, His closeness is less accessible and available to us all.

### Notes

1. Genesis 23:1.

2. Rashi on Genesis 23:1.

3. *The Way of God* 4:4:5.

4. Based on the small *heh* in the word *"behibar'am"* in Genesis 2:4.

5. Rashi on Genesis 2:4.

6. *The Way of God* 4:4:5.

# 7

# "Blessed Is the Name of His Glorious Kingdom Forever and Ever"

The second verse when we say the Shema is "Blessed is the Name of His glorious kingdom forever and ever (*Baruch Shem kevod malchuto le'olam va'ed*)." As was previously mentioned, Jacob was the first person to say this, and he said it on his deathbed when he saw that all of his children had perfect faith in God.[1]

Prior to saying this, Jacob reviewed his life. He had suffered terribly from what seemed, at the time, to be pointless tragedies. He had to flee from his home and parents so that his brother Esau wouldn't kill him. His dishonest father-in-law, who was also his employer, constantly tried to cheat him. Instead of marrying his beloved Rachel after working for her for seven years, he was tricked into first marrying her sister Leah. Rachel died a few years later when she gave birth to their son Benjamin. Jacob's daughter Dinah was raped and kidnapped by a local prince. Two of Jacob's sons then killed all the men of his town. Rachel's older son Joseph was seventeen when his brothers sold him into slavery. Jacob grieved inconsolably for his favorite son for twenty-two years because he was led to believe that Joseph was dead. Toward the end of his life, Jacob thought that he would lose two more of his sons at the hands of the viceroy of Egypt. Finally, a famine forced Jacob to leave the Holy Land and move his entire family to Egypt, a bastion of pagan immorality and depravity.

His suffering aged him so much that when Pharaoh met him, Pharaoh asked how old he was. Jacob responded, "The days of my sojournings are 130 years; few and bad have been the days of the years of my life...."[2] On his deathbed seventeen years later, Jacob had a different perspective about his tribulations. When he saw that all of his troubles were responsible for creating twelve Jewish tribes who had perfect faith in God, he felt exhilarated. With hindsight, he was able to see how all of his experiences had come together in a positive way and had resulted in the formation of an eternal Jewish people.

The spiritual flaws of ancestors tend to show up in their descendants. When Jacob's children lived up to his beliefs, they exemplified his, and their, spiritual greatness. Their assertion, by saying the Shema, of their wholehearted belief in God made Jacob appreciate that even the "bad" events of his life had happened due to God's beneficent providence. With that realization he exclaimed, "Blessed is the Name of His glorious kingdom forever and ever."

The Talmud relates that Jacob said this verse, but Moses did not. It questions whether we should say it, then determines that we should, but in a whisper.[3] A midrash elucidates why.[4] God taught Moses the Oral Law on Mount Sinai after He gave the Jews the Torah. There, Moses heard the angels sing, "Blessed is the Name of His glorious kingdom forever and ever." Moses wanted to bring this proclamation to earth, but was concerned that the angels would call him a thief for bringing to mortals what belonged to celestial beings. In order to avoid that, he determined that Jews should say this verse softly so that the angels couldn't hear it.

But on the Day of Atonement, we proclaim this verse aloud instead of in the customary undertone. We breach daily protocol then because we aren't worried about being termed "thieves" on the holiest day of the year. We will soon see why.

As we mentioned, the first verse of the Shema states our faith that God directs everything toward a meaningful goal that will ultimately be good, although we can't see that now. We accept that on faith because His ways are beyond human comprehension. In fact, that is one reason why we cover our eyes when we say the first verse of the Shema. We proclaim that the Almighty is One, and that everything stems from His love for us and is for a good purpose. Yet we say this while covering our eyes to show that we don't presently see that goodness or unity.

"Blessed is the Name of His glorious kingdom forever and ever" expresses our exhilaration at *seeing* the Master of the World as the source of everything. The verse means that the entire world is nothing more than the presence of the Almighty's kingdom. Seeing Him everywhere draws these words from us.

Thus, the first verse of the Shema expresses belief and faith, while the second states a reality that few mortals experience in this lifetime.

## Perceptions and Reality

When something good happens, we are supposed to say, "Blessed are You, Lord our God, King of the Universe, Who is good and Who does good." When tragedy strikes, such as when a loved one dies, we say, "Blessed are You, Lord our God, King of the Universe, who is the true Judge."[5]

Presently, some things appear good, such as having a lot of money, enjoying good health and longevity, or bringing a baby into the world. Unpleasant things, such as death, pain, suffering, and the like, seem bad. When tragedy strikes, we state our belief in God by declaring Him a true Judge, but we certainly don't rejoice. In the Messianic era, though, we will understand how God only makes unpleasant things happen for positive reasons. Then we will say the blessing that He is good and does good over both painful and joyful occurrences, because we will see clearly how both serve worthwhile purposes. Currently, our perceptions are too clouded by our emotions to see a higher purpose in most painful events.

This is illustrated by a beautiful story:[6]

Rabbi Yehoshua ben Levi asked the Almighty to teach him why righteous people suffer and the wicked prosper. One day, Elijah the Prophet appeared to him and agreed to let the rabbi see how he carried out the Lord's will. But Elijah prefaced their sojourn with the admonition: "You will see many things that will upset you and that you won't understand. You can't ask me to explain what I'm doing or you will have to leave me." The rabbi agreed to the stipulation and they went on their way.

First, they met an old, extremely poor couple who lived in a tiny shack. Their main possession was a single cow.

Despite their abject poverty and cramped quarters, the couple begged the two men to spend the night, and the men agreed. The next morning, having received the couple's warm hospitality, Elijah prayed that God would kill their cow. As the two men were on their way, the rabbi heard the woman scream pitifully from the yard, "Ay! What will we do? Our cow has died!"

That evening, the rabbi and Elijah came to a sumptuous home and knocked on the door. When no one answered, Elijah said, "Let's go in." Inside, a wealthy man and his wife dined on delicacies, and their servants waited on them. Rather than invite the strangers to join them, the man blurted out, "Who let these strangers in? We must be careful to bolt the front door so that people like them don't bother us."

When the guests asked if they might stay the night, the owner reluctantly agreed to let them sleep on a stone bench in the backyard and gave them nothing to eat or drink.

The next morning, Elijah prayed that a damaged wall of the man's house, in imminent danger of collapse, should miraculously be repaired. To the rabbi's amazement, the damage disappeared and the wall looked new in a few moments.

That evening, the men went to a synagogue whose members were very wealthy. Each had his own seat, and strangers didn't dare sit in a member's place. So the two newcomers huddled in a back corner, scorned by the few men who even noticed them. They ended up giving the beadle of the synagogue some money to buy them bread. None of the members offered the guests hospitality.

As they left the next morning, Elijah prayed, "May it be the Lord's will that all of these people be leaders and important people."

By day's end, they reached another city. The people there treated them royally, fed them delicious food, and kept them company. The next morning, Elijah prayed, "May it be the Lord's will that He grant you only one leader."

The rabbi could no longer contain himself. "I don't understand you. You pray for bad things to happen to good people, and for good things to happen to bad people. What are you doing?!"

Elijah replied, "We will have to part company because you broke your promise, but I will explain what I did. The poor man's wife was supposed to die the next day. I prayed that she be spared and that her cow die in her stead. They will suffer for a short time from their loss, but the wife will soon bring home a lot of money and they will live so comfortably that they won't miss the cow.

"Under the rich man's collapsing wall was a cache of gold. Had he repaired it, he would have seen the treasure.

"The wall will soon collapse again, and will be irreparable. By that time, the man will have so many problems, the last thing on his mind will be fixing his house.

"I prayed that the wealthy, selfish snobs in the synagogue should all become leaders. They will always fight with each other because each will want to totally run the town. They will quarrel so much that they will never have any peace.

"I prayed that our last hosts should have only one leader because they will live peacefully with one person they all agree should be in charge.

"All of this goes to show that you can't judge God's ways by what you see. Only He knows if what looks good really is, and if what looks bad really is."

This story reminds us of how distorted our perceptions can be. We express this idea three times a day in the *Aleinu* prayer when we say, "On that day, the Lord will be One and His Name will be One."[7] The Talmud says that *God* is One, but His *Name* is not presently One.[8] Being "One" means that His existence and the way He runs the world are consistent and never change. Even if we know that He runs the world, we *feel* that many other forces control life beside Him. In that regard, His Name is not One now, although that will change when the Messiah comes.

Although we *believe* that God is all-Merciful, we don't always *feel* that way. He does not expect us to pretend that painful experiences feel good, which is why we don't say a blessing acknowledging Him as all-good when tragedy strikes. Blessings must express how we truly feel, and we are not yet at a point where we feel good when unpleasant things happen. When we hurt, we must fall back on a reservoir of faith and state that God is a judge who acts fairly, not deny our emotions and proclaim His goodness.

This is why we say aloud, "Hear, Israel, the Lord is our God, the Lord is One." We state a belief in God that our forefathers have passed down to us from generation to generation. This foundation of faith has carried us through many difficult moments when God's goodness and presence seem hidden. We won't see God's total goodness until our souls enter the afterlife, or during the Messianic era. For now, we have to accept God's total goodness on faith.

"Blessed is the Name of His glorious kingdom forever and ever" declares that we see *only* God's unity. Since that is not the case now, we cannot yet say this verse without qualification. The fact that Jacob said it means that it is possible to reach this spiritual level. Were we never to say it, we would rule out the possibility of ever attaining his spiritual peak. That would be inappropriate since all of history is advancing toward a time when we will see only God's goodness everywhere. On the other hand, it would be presumptuous to say it aloud now since we don't feel its truth in our hearts. Jacob could say this verse without hesitation because he saw God's "Oneness" with total clarity. We are not at his level, although that will change in the future.

We resolve this dilemma by compromising. We say the verse in a whisper, reflecting the fact that we will ultimately see its truth, but not presently.

Angels can exclaim, "Blessed is the Name of His glorious kingdom forever and ever" because they aren't confused by the goings-on of the physical world. They exist in a realm where they only see God's infinite light, wisdom, power, and goodness everywhere, and are awed by His greatness. They always know with total clarity that He only does good, so they can loudly proclaim this verse every day. They don't say the Shema's first verse because it expresses faith, and they don't need faith to appreciate the idea that He is One. It is always evident to them.

Angels see no disparity between what God is and how He operates in their world. They aren't physical, so nothing exists for them except God's will. They can't say, as we do, "God, I want to have my own life and do my own thing." They never know the tension of being commanded to do what God wants while having competing desires.

We certainly don't feel as connected to our Creator as angels do. We are constantly distracted by pleasures and temptations that have nothing to do with His will. We live in a confusing world where right and wrong, good and bad, aren't always apparent. But one day a year, on the Day of Atonement (Yom Kippur), we transcend the physical world and  emerge from its confusion. For twenty-five hours, we resemble angels, and can proclaim aloud as they do, "Blessed is the Name of His glorious kingdom forever and ever." On that day, we surpass the angels by elevating ourselves above the challenges of the physical world.

We proclaim our *faith* in God's unity because we can't usually feel and see it. Saying "Blessed is the Name of His glorious kingdom forever and ever" really contradicts our human natures. We are "stealing" the angels' "script" because only they can truthfully say that they constantly feel and see God's unity. They connect to the Almighty by saying "Blessed is His Name...." We connect through the faith and belief of "Hear, Israel, the Lord is our God, the Lord is One." On the Day of Atonement, though, we transcend the confusion of the physical world. The angels can honestly say their verse the entire year; we can only do so on Yom Kippur when we reach their level.

As Jacob's descendants, we can also feel some of his excitement when we recognize God's unity. When we whisper, "Blessed is the Name of His glorious kingdom...," we aspire to someday attain Jacob's spiritual height. In the meantime, we proclaim the angels' verse without hesitation the one day a year that we reach their level.

## Indelible Marks of Spirituality

When God gave us the Torah on Mount Sinai 3,300 years ago, Moses stayed with Him on the mountain, learning the Oral Law. The Israelites miscalculated when he was supposed to return; and they thought he had died when he did not come back on time. They reacted by building a golden calf to symbolize a replacement leader. Moses and God knew that Moses would smash the tablets engraved with the Ten Commandments when he came down from the mountain and saw what they had done. Still, he "convinced" God to let him bring the tablets down, anyway.

The Ten Commandments represent the unification of the spiritual and physical worlds. Moses hoped that bringing their tangible representation into our world for even an instant would help the Israelites reach a spiritual level that would enable them to properly receive a second set of Ten Commandments. And, in fact, after Moses smashed the first set, their being here once made it easier for the Jews to accept the second set.

During the forty years they lived in the Sinai wilderness, the Israelites were protected by special clouds. A special well provided them with water, and they ate manna. The Talmud says that each of these gifts occurred in someone's merit. The manna fell in Moses' merit, the water was due to his sister Miriam's merit, and the protective clouds were because of their brother Aaron's merit.

When Miriam died, the well ceased, but her brothers' merits brought it back. When Aaron died, the clouds and the well both ceased, but Moses' merit reinstated them. Finally, when Moses died, the clouds, the well, and the manna all stopped.

It might seem that the clouds and the well could have started in Moses' merit if he was able to reinstate them. Yet the Shelah Hakadosh, a commentator on the Torah, says that only Miriam could bring down the spiritual energy that initiated having a miraculous well. Once she did that, others could reinstate it. The same applied to Aaron's drawing down the spiritual energy for the protective clouds. They only needed to be reacquired when they disappeared. Reacquiring something is not nearly as difficult as creating it *de novo*.

The Talmud expresses a similar idea by saying that a fetus learns the entire Torah *in utero*, then forgets it at birth. Why bother having a nine-month course of study where the student forgets everything at the end?

The answer is that although we have no conscious memories of our earliest Torah learning, we tap into our unconscious knowledge when we relearn it and reawaken what we once knew.

In similar fashion, Jacob and his children gave us a deep reservoir of faith in God, plus the ability to see His unity in our daily lives. Once they brought them into our world, they have been our gifts for all time.

## Notes

1. Genesis 49:1.
2. Ibid. 47:9.
3. *Pesachim* 56a.
4. *Devarim Rabbah* 2:36.
5. *Pesachim* 50a. This blessing may also be translated, "...the Judge of the truth."
6. From *Yalkut Sippurim,* quoting from *Sefer Hama'asiyot* of Rabbeinu Nissim Gaon.
7. *Zechariah* 14:9.
8. *Pesachim* 50a.

# 8

# The First Paragraph of the Shema

Each of the three paragraphs that comprise the Shema has a specific theme. The first portion's theme is our acceptance of God's government and our commitment to serve Him.[1] The theme of the second portion is our willingness to do mitzvot, which represent the duties of our King's government[2] and are the means by which we develop an ongoing relationship with Him. The third portion's theme is our remembering the Jews' Exodus from Egypt and men's requirement to wear fringes ("tzitzit") on their four-cornered garments. The Exodus represents the Almighty's involvement in and control of history, His ability to do miracles, and our commitment to maintain the spiritual achievements that we made when we left Egypt.

The order of these three sections does not follow their order in the Torah. The third portion appears first, in the book of Numbers, while the first two sections appear subsequently in the book of Deuteronomy. We will soon see why the Shema was purposely constructed in non-chronological order.

## Loving God

The first section of the Shema says, "You should love the Lord your God with all of your heart, and with all of your soul, and with all of your resources."[3] This commands us to love God, yet how can He dictate our emotions? A commandment should tell us to do something that is in our control. How can God expect us to control how we feel?

The answer is that we actually have much more control over our emotions than we think. We change our feelings by focusing on specific events or ideas that make us feel a certain way. We can also do certain actions, or expose ourselves to certain experiences, that result in our having the kinds of emotions that we want to have.

For example, marriage counselors know that couples who do nothing loving for each other soon lose their feelings for one another. The more each spouse does for a partner, the more loving the doer feels.

The relationship between God and us can be analogized to a relationship between people. When two people don't feel loving towards each other, they create loving feelings by doing what the other person likes. The more each gives of his energy, time, and resources, the more he or she will love the recipient of the giving. Not only does love result in giving, giving results in love.

We normally have barriers of "self" that separate us from others. The more we give others our time, energy, and resources, the more we break down our walls of separation. That makes us less preoccupied with what is "ours" versus what is "theirs." The more we take down these walls, the less we see others as distinct from us, and instead see them as extensions of ourselves.

This is why our Sages said that the way to develop love for others is to remove the barriers of "self" that divide us. We do this by giving of ourselves and doing for others.

We create love for God in a similar way. We grow to love Him by committing our heart, spirit, and resources to doing what He wants of us. The degree to which we give ourselves to God is the extent to which we end up loving Him.

For example, imagine spending $50 on special food for the Sabbath, on a *lulav* and *etrog* for Sukkot (the holiday of Tabernacles), or on any other mitzvah. If we do it solely because our relationship to God is very precious, and He has asked us to do this, our act breaks down part of our "self" at His request. In turn, this begins the process of identifying with the Almighty. We stop seeing our desires and personality as separate from His. His desires become an extension of our desires, and we start to love Him.

The Shema says that Jews should love God with all of their "*levavcha*,"[4] instead of using the Hebrew word "*libcha*," meaning "your heart." The two letters *bet* in the word *levavcha* mean that we should love God with "both hearts." In other words, we should serve Him with both of our inclinations, the one that wants to do good things and the one that wants us to go against His will.[5]

Our good inclination motivates us to do God's will. We might assume that it would automatically motivate us to follow the Torah's directives, but that is not necessarily the case. It can also encourage us to do things that we perceive as good or that feel good, but aren't, because they don't serve God. For instance, some people are very compassionate by nature. They can be kind to others because it feels right or comfortable to be that way, not because that's what God wants under the circumstances. Serving the Almighty with our positive inclination means that even if something "feels" right, our ultimate reason for doing it is that it is His will. We shouldn't do things simply because we want to do them. We should do them because that is what God wants of us.

How do we serve our Creator with our negative inclination? When it draws us to do the opposite of what He wants, we can channel those impulses constructively. For instance, if we have a tremendous desire to eat non-kosher food, we can find a kosher substitute, and eat it as a special treat on the Sabbath or on a Jewish festival. If we want public honor, we can give money to a charity and have our name put on a plaque for all to see. If we have a desire to gossip, we can visit sick patients in a hospital and chat with them in beneficial ways. These are all ways of channeling negative feelings into serving God.

The One Above does not want us to totally deny our desires. They are part of our individuality, and it would be very destructive to deny our uniqueness. Rather, all of our endowments and yearnings have a proper venue for expression within God's will, and we are repeatedly challenged to find them.

At times, we may need to repress certain negative desires that we are not experienced enough, or strong enough, to channel properly. In the meantime, we may need to strengthen our positive convictions and behaviors before we can control and channel our negative feelings properly. That keeps us from being controlled by inappropriate desires.

Serving God with "both" hearts doesn't mean that we serve Him instead of serving our negative inclinations. It means that when we serve the Almighty, we harness our positive and negative drives simultaneously. None of our feelings stands apart from a relationship with our Creator.

The Shema recognizes that we often have competing desires. We can't have a deep relationship with God if we have one foot out the door, with part of us running away from Him. We have to find some way of appropriately expressing all of our feelings within a relationship to Him.

We are supposed to feel love for God when we say the first paragraph of the Shema, and not be detached subjects in His kingdom. We try to devote wholeheartedly to Him whatever we have to offer. One person will dedicate his zest for living, another will dedicate his money to serving His Maker, a third will dedicate her gift of speech, and so on. We must be prepared to dedicate everything we have to serving God.

## *With All of Your Soul*

The Shema tells us to love God with all of our "soul."[6] That means that we should be prepared to give up our lives rather than renounce our belief in God.[7] We should feel that life is not worth living unless we can have a totally committed relationship to our Creator.

When we say the Shema, we are supposed to be willing to give up our lives to defend God's unity. This is almost as spiritually beneficial as actually giving up our lives to sanctify His Name, because they both show our belief in Him.[8]

Throughout history, Christians and other groups made Jews choose to die as martyrs if they were not willing to renounce their belief in God. Even the most simple, "unsophisticated" Jews endured terrible tortures and death rather than compromise their belief in one, true God.

Since World War II, Jews have rarely faced this test. Why, then, should we imagine forfeiting our lives for God when we are unlikely ever to have to do so? And can we honestly say that we would do it if we had the choice?

The reason we imagine sanctifying God in the ultimate way is because we cannot grow without dreaming and imagining. Jews cannot live only in the here and now. We must harbor hopes for the future. Hoping and dreaming about spiritual mountains to conquer motivates us to fulfill our potential.

Rabbi Tzaddok HaCohen said that every Jew's spiritual dreams are within his or her reach. Were they not, the person's soul wouldn't thirst for them, and he or she wouldn't have those dreams. Every time we dream of ascending a spiritual height, it means that our soul silently yearns to achieve that goal. We need to take such dreams seriously because they are windows into our souls' yearnings.

Dreams, then, help us actualize ourselves by suggesting goals and giving us insight into our deepest spiritual desires.

While dreams can be powerful motivators of spiritual growth, poorly directed imagination can be self-destructive. Fantasizing negative thoughts is far from harmless. It creates spiritual entities that harm our souls.

Our thoughts and emotions, the workings of our hearts and minds, can build or destroy our inner selves. "Eating ourselves up" with our ruminations is more than just a figure of speech. Obsessions can destroy us more than any actions can.

Judaism is a religion of action that exhorts us to express our religious beliefs by the way we live. We can't truly believe in God only with our minds. Our thoughts must be backed by actions.

Yet God is also concerned with our strivings, hopes, and imagination. They affect a critical part of our souls, so we shouldn't dismiss their importance and power. The acid test of how much we really believe something is what we are willing to do to demonstrate that belief.

Rabbi Moshe Chaim Luzzatto said that a Jew can only believe in God if he translates belief into behaviors that express his convictions. When we contemplate giving up our lives for God every time that we say the Shema, we are supposed to feel that we cannot live meaningfully without Jewish values and beliefs. If we can imagine living without them, our beliefs cannot be terribly precious. A belief system that is dispensable cannot be supreme.

When a Jew actually gives up his or her life to sanctify God's Name, that behavior expresses convictions that bring tremendous and awesome holiness into this world.[9] Survivors can then build upon and grow from this gift. After World War II, the world seemed spiritually empty, but it was not. All the Jews throughout history who forfeited their lives because they were Jewish left behind permanent holiness by virtue of the statement their deaths made.

Every day we can choose to elevate or lower ourselves spiritually. God asks us to spend our lives sanctifying His Name every day, by making Him our central focus. Saying the Shema with this idea in mind recharges the world's spiritual batteries, creates holiness, and draws the world out of its darkness. In other words, committing ourselves to the idea of giving up our lives for God without actually doing it corrects the world spiritually.[10]

If we live only for truth, we won't renounce it even if someone puts a gun to our head and demands that we give up our faith. Judaism urges us to come to terms with what we're living for, without being forced to choose between life and our beliefs. As long as we can imagine living without Judaism, we are not willing to die for its ideals.

We internalize the right beliefs by developing a deep appreciation for how the Torah system of life works, and then living by its principles. The more we learn about it and attach ourselves to it, the less we can imagine living without it.

For example, many Jews from secular backgrounds once thought that they would never get to a point of observing the Sabbath. A year later, they couldn't imagine how they ever *didn't* keep the Sabbath! This is but one illustration of how we cannot live without Judaism.

This is what Rabbi Luzzatto meant when he said that a Jew should imagine giving up his life for God when he says the Shema.[11] If we truly appreciate how precious Judaism is, we will never give it up and will automatically want to dedicate our lives to God. Those who feel what a Jewish life is truly supposed to be never want to let it go.

## With All of Your Money

The Shema says that we should love the Lord with all of our financial resources (*meodecha*).[12] Among other things, this means that we should be willing to spend a percentage of our money on the performance of mitzvot.

A Jew may say that he loves God, but really love money more. As long as loving the Almighty doesn't cost anything, he will love Him. As soon it requires giving 10 percent of his money to charity, spending money on religious articles, and paying a small premium for kosher food, he will be less committed to a relationship with God.

Our Sages noted that the order in the Shema of how to love God is with "all your heart, soul, and money." We would think that someone who is ready to give up his life for God would automatically love Him with his money. Though this is true for many people, this sequence teaches that some feel their money is more dear to them than their lives.[13] During the Depression, for example, some people committed suicide rather than live in poverty.

The Shema addresses both types of people. A person who loves life more than anything, including money, is required to give his life in the service of loving God. Someone who loves money more than anything else, even life itself, must dedicate his money to loving the One Above. We are all required to dedicate what we hold most dear to loving our Maker. Being truly devoted and dedicated to Him means that we hold nothing back from Him. We should be prepared to do anything and everything necessary to show our love for Him, including dedicating to His service what we treasure most.

It is interesting how many people are willing to dedicate their emotions, and even many of their actions, to serving God. But as soon as they have to be so ethical in business that they will apparently lose money; or they can't work on the Sabbath or Jewish holidays; or they must give money to charity or spend it on Jewish education for their children, their dedication stops.

The Shema tells us that it costs money to have a relationship with God. We accept that it costs money to develop and sustain a relationship between people. Singles spend money on a date. Married men buy a spouse and children clothes, food, presents, and the like. Business people spend money to take associates out for meals and entertainment.

For some reason, people think that having a relationship with God should be free. Much to their chagrin, Jewish organizations and teachers repeatedly find that Jews will spend untold thousands of dollars to buy and furnish beautiful homes, acquire expensive cars, and go on luxury vacations. They think that going out to restaurants and owning designer clothes are necessities. Many Jews save money for decades so that they can put their children through college. Yet when it comes to paying a few thousand dollars for their children to get a Torah education, or when it costs a few dollars to enroll in Jewish adult education classes or pay membership fees to belong to a synagogue, they balk and complain about the price. They expect their children's Ivy League education to set them back tens of thousands of dollars while expecting quality Jewish education to be free.

We can't break the barriers of "self" that keep us from being close to God if we aren't willing to spend money on our relationship with Him.

## Put These Words on Your Heart

After the Shema tells us to love God wholeheartedly, it says, "And these words that I command you today should be on your heart."[14] These "words" refer to loving the One Above by dedicating both "parts" of our heart, our entire soul, and our financial resources to Him. We must first invest ourselves fully in our relationship with Him before we can love Him. Even though we won't initially feel that we are acting out of love for God, we will eventually love Him intensely and give of ourselves if we commit ourselves totally to Him.

The Shema tells us to put its words *"al levavecha."*[15] This literally means "on your heart." The Chassidic masters tell us that we frequently feel emotionally estranged from God. At best, we might be intellectually aware that a deity exists, but feel no emotional closeness to Him. We might be willing to do what God asks of us as long as we feel close to Him, but not when the relationship doesn't feel emotionally gratifying.

This attitude is especially common when we pray. We may be fortunate enough to be inspired by an intense awareness of God's presence once in a while. Most of the time when we pray, we feel no connection at all, and we just can't "get into" praying. That feeling keeps many people from communicating with the Almighty.

Judaism says that it is normal to feel spiritually estranged more often than not. We can still grow even when we feel far from God, as long as we keep working on our spirituality regardless of how we feel. If we stop acting the right way, we will be in the "wrong place" when our hearts do open to our Heavenly Father, and we may be unable to capitalize on our receptivity to Him at those precious moments.

This is why we are supposed to discipline ourselves, regardless of how we feel, to always keep these words "on" our hearts. When we are spiritually open, that attitude lets us maximize opportunities that present themselves to grow closer to the Almighty.

When our heart is not open to the One Above, and we put things on top of it, whatever is piled up there will fall in when our heart does open.[16] Spiritual growth requires us to "pile up" as much effort as we can, even when our efforts don't seem to amount to much. Then, in our moments of spiritual receptivity, we will be ready to reap the rewards of our sustained discipline.

This part of the Shema tells how we can get to a point of loving God: by working hard and dedicating what we have to serving Him. It also tells us what to do when we don't yet feel consistent love for Him: to serve Him even when we don't feel like it. Without consistent self-discipline, we can't develop the love that is a foundation of our relationship with God. We need to know that none of our spiritual efforts is ever wasted. Sooner or later, our efforts will bear fruit.

A mature relationship with God, or with people, requires love, responsibility, and an ability to delay gratification. It is easy for two people to act lovingly when they feel close. But feelings wax and wane, so couples need to act consistently loving even when they don't feel like it. For example, if a husband is angry, he should still do what a loving man does for a wife, and vice versa. Otherwise, doing only what we feel guarantees that we will ruin our marriage. On the other hand, disciplining ourselves to act lovingly regardless of how we feel maximizes the effects of our good feelings when we are emotionally receptive to a spouse.

Discipline can be uncomfortable, yet it allows us to give to, and receive from, a spouse during difficult times. It also keeps a relationship from breaking down. Discipline lets us take away our barriers of "self" that otherwise make it impossible to identify with, and do for, a spouse when we aren't so inclined.

## The Mitzvah of Teaching Torah

After telling us to "put these words on your heart," the Shema says, "And you should teach them (*v'shinantam*) to your children."[17] The Talmud says that *v'shinantam* means that a parent should teach Torah to his children with clarity and vibrancy.[18] The mandate to teach Torah to one's children also includes students, who are considered their teachers' children.[19] This is because teachers give "birth" to their students by endowing them with spiritual life. The obligation to "teach Torah to your children" means that we should teach those to whom we can give a new meaning and context to life.

It is customary at Jewish weddings for parents to walk the bride and groom down the aisle to the wedding canopy. A famous rabbi maintained that the groom's spiritual father, his rebbe, should also accompany them. He wanted people to see that the relationship between a Torah teacher and his student is like that of a parent and child, not that of a secular teacher and student. The Torah teacher gives his students a form of life and a context in which to live it. He does not simply give book knowledge.

Many great Sages never had children, and their disciples were considered to be their children. For example, the prophet Elijah's greatest disciple was Elisha. When Elijah left this world, he ascended to heaven in a fiery chariot. When Elisha witnessed this miraculous scene, he exclaimed, "My father, my father, chariot of Israel...."[20]

Elijah was not Elisha's biological father. Elisha called him "father" because Elijah enriched Elisha's spiritual life by being his religious teacher and mentor.

This idea is further borne out by Jewish law. For example, if one's spiritual mentor and one's father must be redeemed after being taken captive, redeeming the spiritual teacher takes precedence.

Once we dedicate ourselves fully to the One Above, we

will want to transmit our feelings to our children. Liberal parents often want their children to make personal religious choices without the parents telling them what to do. These same parents are quite willing to make sure that their children learn to swim, ski, play tennis and other sports, play piano and dance, visit museums, go to the theater and watch movies, and learn about non-Jewish cultures. The parents don't say, "Let my children discover these things when they grow up. I don't want to inflict my enjoyment of these activities on them."

Jewish parents with unhealthy attitudes find Judaism burdensome, and they are reluctant to "inflict" Judaism on their offspring. Parents who truly love God and treasure their relationship with Him want those they love also to enjoy this wonderful gift.

This is a major difference between having a personalized relationship with our Heavenly Father versus having only a sense of obligation. If we truly feel, not only believe, that a relationship with God makes life worth living, we can't help but want the same for our children. This is why as soon as the Shema states the importance of loving God, it commands us to convey these same feelings to our children:

> And you should love the Lord your God with all of your heart, with all of your soul, and with all of your resources. And these words that I command you today should be on your heart. And you should teach them to your children....[21]

If we treasure Judaism as much as we value our material heirlooms and money, we will want our children to have these same spiritual delights, not only share our material ones.

A litmus test of parents' feelings toward God is their desire to teach Judaism to their children. If parents spend a lot of time and effort doing this, their relationship with their Creator is obviously precious. Unfortunately, few Jewish parents today love God. At best, many of them do religious rituals by rote. This sets a terrible example for children because their greatest education is seeing that their parents love Judaism and feel fulfilled living by its rules and perspectives. If children would only see their parents' lives revolving around Judaism, the children would want to discover its beauty for themselves.

The Shema obligates a father to teach his sons Torah.[22] The Talmud says that this obligation requires a parent not to hesitate when he teaches.[23] Hesitating shows that he is not completely connected to Torah, or that his understanding is incomplete. Every parent should learn Torah to a point that it flows naturally from him, with love and pride, when he transmits it to the next generation.

A rabbi once asked a student to explain an idea to him. The student replied that he understood the concept but couldn't explain it. The rabbi responded, "If you can't explain it, you don't truly understand it."

The Shema requires parents to have intellectual, as well as behavioral, clarity when they transmit Torah to their children. They should not give mixed messages that the Torah says one thing while they model something else.

Parents often teach their children to do as they say, not as they do! When parents teach Judaism this way, children get confused. They can only learn Torah properly when the verbal lessons are consistent with the teacher's model.

## Discussing Torah

The Shema continues, "And you shall speak of them [words of Torah] when you sit in your house, and when you go on the way, and when you lie down, and when you rise up."[24] We tend to talk about what is most important to us. For example, a newly engaged couple will talk incessantly about their wedding plans. A couple with a new baby will go on and on about the labor, delivery, and the infant. Businessmen immerse themselves in conversations about the stock market and finances, and so on.

If Torah is truly important to us, discussions about it should be a major part of what we speak about. We should not relegate Torah to classes or occasional Sabbath meals. We should constantly talk about its ideas when we "sit at home, walk along the way, lie down, and rise up." We should be as preoccupied with Torah as we are about other things that excite us.

## Love God Everywhere

The first portion of the Shema tells us not to relegate our love for God to the synagogue. Unfortunately, many secular Jews today associate being Jewish with attending the synagogue. Synagogue worship was never meant to be more than a small fraction of how Judaism was supposed to be lived. We need to be cognizant of the fact that when we are home, God is there. When we are out socializing, He is there. When we travel, He is there. He is in our workplace and goes with us on vacation. We can only properly teach Judaism to our children if we live with an ongoing consciousness of God's presence. That is why the Shema tells us to teach Judaism to our children, then tells us to put the Shema's words on our doorposts:

And you should teach them to your children, and speak of them when you sit in your house, and when you go on the way...and write them on the [mezuzot that are affixed to the] doorposts of your house and in your gates.[25]

Our homes are overt statements of our relationship with our Sponsor.

We don't restrict our mention of other loving relationships to a few moments a day, nor do we hide our devotion behind closed doors. We show signs of our love everywhere. We put our loved ones' pictures on our desk, display them on our walls, and keep them in our wallet. We leave cards, gifts, and mementos around for all the world to see. When we travel, we don't suddenly forget about our loved ones, either.

The Shema expresses this same idea. We are supposed to discuss Torah when we travel, when we are at home, when we are with our children, and so on. Our love for God should not begin as soon as we enter the synagogue, nor stop as soon as we set foot outside of it. We should always take it with us, and testify to that love in our homes.

We have a constant obligation to love the Almighty, whether we are at home, going places, waking up in the morning, or going to sleep at night, as the Shema says: "...and you should speak of them when you sit in your house, and when you go on the way, and when you lie down, and when you rise up."[26]

### Notes

1. In Hebrew, this is known as *"kabbalat ol Malchut Shamayim."* We do this when we read Deuteronomy 6:4–9.

2. Deuteronomy 11:13–21. This is known as *"kabbalat ol mitzvot."*

3. Deuteronomy 6:5.

4. Ibid.

5. *Berachot* 54a.

6. Deuteronomy 6:5.

7. *Berachot* 54a.

8. *The Way of God* 4:4:5.

9. Ibid.

10. Ibid.

11. Ibid.

12. Deuteronomy 6:5.

13. *Berachot* 61b.

14. Deuteronomy 6:6.

15. Ibid.

16. From Rabbi Menachem Mendel of Kotzk.

17. Deuteronomy 6:7.

18. The Sages in *Kiddushin* 30a described what this entails.

19. Rashi on Deuteronomy 6:7.

20. II Kings 2:13.

21. Deuteronomy 6:5–7.

22. While not commanded to do so, mothers historically have taught Judaism to young children of both sexes, and have continued to teach their daughters until adulthood how to be proper Jews.

23. *Kiddushin* 30a.

24. Deuteronomy 6:7.

25. Ibid. 6:7, 9.

26. Ibid. 6:7.

# 9

## Tefillin

A nd you should bind them as a sign on your hand, and they should be tefillin between your eyes. And write them on the doorposts of your house and in your gates."[1]

We are not supposed to give the Shema mere lip service. We must take it to heart by acting on the beliefs that it professes. Men do this, in part, by tying words of Torah onto their arm and head in the form of tefillin. All Jews do this by living in dwellings that have kosher mezuzot on the doorposts.

Tefillin consist of four Torah selections, written with ink on parchment. The four sections contain verses that 1. profess God's unity, 2. accept the yoke of Heaven, 3. accept the obligation to do God's commandments, with the understanding that we are rewarded for doing them and punished for transgressing them, and 4. remember the Exodus from Egypt.

Moses received oral instruction from God about how to make tefillin.[2] The parchment on which the Torah verses are written is wrapped in a piece of cloth, then in the hair of a kosher animal. It is then placed in a leather box. The box must be square, and it is stitched with the sinews of a kosher animal.

## Symbolisms of Tefillin

The unusual construction of tefillin is very symbolic. They are made from an animal to symbolize that we can only perfect our souls by elevating our animalistic drives, which happens when we do commandments with our bodies. This is our main point of connection to our Creator. Having the right beliefs, thoughts, and feelings is not enough to actualize our spiritual potentials.

Tefillin must come from a kosher animal. Such animals are not inherently holy, but can potentially be made holy if we use them in a way that serves God. Non-kosher animals may not be used because their holy "sparks" are bound in a way that we are unable to actualize their potentials.[3]

Tefillin express man's ability to find God in the physical world, and tying tefillin onto the body represents tying the physical world to the spiritual world. It reminds us not to divorce one from the other. The tefillin even form Hebrew letters that allude to this. The box has a folded border at each end so that a black leather strap can be passed through it. The strap of the head-tefillin is then knotted in the form of the Hebrew letter *dalet*, while the strap of the hand-tefillin forms the letter *yud*. The box worn on the head has the Hebrew letter *shin* on its right and left sides. Together, these letters spell the Hebrew divine name, *Sha-dai*. This name refers to the Almighty stopping Creation at a point where its physicality would still allow people to find Him, instead of totally hiding His presence.

The short calf-hairs that bind the parchments of the

head-tefillin symbolize evil. The hairs are threaded through a small opening in the parchment box so that they can be seen from the outside. Hair comes from something alive, although hair itself is dead. This alludes to the idea that evil's original source is from God. He created evil so that we could be challenged to go against His wishes, then earn reward by choosing to serve Him. The existence of evil allows us to have true free will by tempting us to do what we want instead of what God wants.

But God did not want us to strengthen evil by giving it vitality. The hair on the tefillin reminds us that the strength of evil was initially only that of a hair. The more we choose to go against God's will, the more power and credibility we give evil.

Head-tefillin symbolize God's purpose for the world. The hairs on it teach that all evil can have a holy purpose if we use our free will to reject evil, and choose to act godly.[4]

Inasmuch as tefillin symbolize man's commitment to God, the strap of the hand-tefillin is wrapped around the middle finger like a wedding ring that the Almighty puts on His beloved's hand.[5] The man verbalizes this by saying, "And I will betroth you to Me forever, and I will betroth you to Me with righteousness, and with justice, and with lovingkindness, and with compassion. And I will betroth you to Me with faith and you shall know the Lord."[6]

While hand-tefillin help us act properly, head-tefillin help us properly channel our thoughts and ideas. Ideas are holier than actions because actions belong to the physical world, while ideas are more related to the spiritual world. This is why one may not exchange the box for the head-tefillin with the box that encases the hand-tefillin.[7] The head box is holier, so we can't reduce its holiness. (We may, however, elevate a hand-box into a head-box if need be.)

The head-tefillin are not put on before the hand-tefillin, nor are they worn without hand-tefillin[8] (unless someone has no hand-tefillin). This is why hand-tefillin are not fully removed before the head-tefillin are taken off.[9] Not wearing head-tefillin alone symbolizes our repudiation of the idea that we will do mitzvot (putting on the hand-tefillin) when our ideology (represented by the head-tefillin) is developed enough and we fully understand the rationale for doing each mitzvah.

The hand-tefillin's box faces the heart, while the straps extend down and wrap around the hand. This symbolizes that spiritual actions (the hand) should be done with feeling (facing the heart), not be discharged in an emotionless or rote way. Our actions influence our thoughts, and through them, we build our ideology. Actions with little meaning cannot build significant belief systems.

When a man wears arm-tefillin, it transmits the spiritual awareness to his heart that he loves God, and that God loves him. When he puts tefillin on his head, it sensitizes him to divine providence and strengthens his eyes and senses to serve Him alone. Certain parts of our bodies spiritually nurture the rest of us, and the heart and mind are two such points. God put spiritual qualities into commandments so that they will protect the parts of us that do them. Otherwise, our limbs will be easily seduced by the world's temptations.

The head-tefillin have four chambers, while the hand-tefillin have only one.[10] This symbolizes how many senses each tefillin helps sanctify. The head has four senses: smell, sight, hearing, and taste, which are elevated by the four chambers of the head-tefillin. The hand has but one sense, touch, which we elevate through the one chamber of the hand-tefillin. Since we perceive the physical world through our five senses, and the purpose of life is to sanctify the physical world, wearing tefillin helps us do that.

The head-tefillin contains four sections of verses from the Torah, each of which mentions that its words should be placed in the tefillin. The first two sections contain the Shema and our acceptance of God's commandments ("And it shall be, if you listen..."). These express our recognition of God and His having communicated commandments to us. The other two portions of the head-tefillin discuss the Exodus from Egypt and the sanctification of the first-born. We sanctify the first-born of animals and first-born Jewish boys because God saved our first-born males in Egypt and destroyed those of the Egyptians.

Everything that is first is holy. Sanctifying our first-born, just as we sanctify our first fruits and first shearing of the sheep, shows our willingness to dedicate the best of what we have to God.

## Wearing Tefillin

Now that we understand something about the symbolism that underlies the construction of tefillin, we can discuss how and when they are used.

Every morning, men place the leather boxes containing the parchments onto their heads and arms, wrapping the arm-tefillin's strap around their forearms.

A right-handed man places the arm-tefillin on his left bicep,[11] facing his heart. He then puts on the head-*tefillin* after saying the following prayer:

Behold, when I put on tefillin, I intend to fulfill my Creator's command, Who commanded us to put on tefillin, as it is written in His Torah: 'And you should bind them as a sign on your hand, and they should be tefillin between your eyes.' And these four portions [of the Torah, written on the tefillin parchments], 'Hear...[the first paragraph of the Shema],' 'And it shall be, if you listen...[the second paragraph of the Shema],' 'Sanctify...,' and 'It will be when you come...' have within them the oneness and unity of the Blessed One of the world, so that we will remember the miracles and wonders that He did for us when He took us out of Egypt; and to Whom belongs strength and rulership in the worlds above and below to do with as He wishes. He commanded us to put [tefillin] on the hand, to remember the outstretched arm [of God during the plagues and the Exodus from Egypt]. It is opposite the heart, to subdue the desires and thoughts of our heart for His service, may His Name be blessed. [And we put tefillin] on the head opposite the brain, so that my soul in my brain, with my other senses and abilities, will all be subjugated to His service, may His Name be blessed. And may the influence of the commandment of tefillin be extended upon me so that I have a long life, and a flow of holiness, and holy thoughts without ideas of any unintentional or intentional sin. Let us not be seduced nor incited by the evil inclination, and let us be left to serve the Lord with our hearts. And may it be Your will, Lord our God and God of our forefathers, that this commandment of putting on tefillin be important before the Holy One, blessed is He, as if I had fulfilled it with all of its details, specifics, and intentions, as well as the 613 commandments that depend upon it. Amen Selah.

Tefillin have tremendous sanctity, and wearing them acts as a conduit for bringing enormous spiritual energy into this world. Due to this sanctity, they may not be worn if a man's body is not clean, and it is assumed that men will not have the requisite holy thoughts and cleanliness to wear them any longer than is necessary.[12] Normally, parents start training children to do other commandments from the time the children are three years old, although they are not fully obligated to do mitzvot until boys are bar mitzvah (thirteen years and a day old) and girls are bat mitzvah (twelve years and a day old). With respect to tefillin, however, Ashkenazic boys start wearing them a month or so before their bar mitzvah, while Sephardim may begin a year or more in advance. This minimizes the chances that they will wear tefillin in an improper state.

The concern with wearing tefillin only in a holy state is relevant to adult men as well. In ancient times, Torah scholars and saintly men wore tefillin throughout the day, but today tefillin are rarely worn outside of the morning prayers.[13]

It is important for Jewish boys to know how to put on tefillin properly as soon they as they reach Jewish adulthood so that they don't miss even a day. Every day that a Jewish man neglects to wear tefillin as required, he transgresses eight positive commandments.[14]

Despite all of the commandments that are fulfilled by wearing tefillin, they are not worn on the Sabbath or Jewish holidays because they are a "sign" of the special bond

between God and the Jews.[15] The Sabbath and Jewish
holidays are also "signs,"[16] so wearing tefillin on those days
is superfluous.[17]

Our Sages said that the Jewish people and God made four
pacts regarding every mitzvah in the Torah: to learn about
them, to teach them, to guard them so that they will
always be performed, and to do them.[18] While women are
not obligated to wear tefillin and tzitzit, they can have as
much a part of these mitzvot as men by learning about
them, teaching others how to do them, and protecting
them. In other words, while men are required to wear
tefillin and tzitzit,[19] both men and women can create a
relationship with the Almighty using some or all of the
aspects of these mitzvot.

Women can also accomplish these effects using totally
different means. What men accomplish by wearing tefillin,
women accomplish by creating new Jewish lives through
giving birth and making a Jewish home. Thus, the box of the
hand-tefillin is analogous to the womb, and its strap symbolizes the umbilical cord. The word for box in Hebrew, *bayit*, also
means "home." When a woman creates a Jewish home that is
permeated with Torah, it is similar to the box of the tefillin
that contains Torah words, which is tied to the body.[20]

## Spiritual Roots of Tefillin

The Jews in Egypt identified with the unholiness that the
Egyptians lived and breathed. When God redeemed our
ancestors, they got back the spiritual greatness that they had
lost during their lengthy stay in Egypt. That is why the book
of Exodus ends with the building of the Tabernacle. The
consummation of the Jews' redemption occurred when they

had a tangible representation that God dwelled in their midst. Redemption from Egypt means that the Jews redis-covered buried treasures within themselves that had been in a state of "captivity."

Due to God's revelation during the Ten Plagues, the Israelites sang holy songs the night of the Exodus de-spite having slipped to the forty-ninth level of spiritual impurity. They did this by identifying with a more impor-tant life force than unholiness, and realizing that God's will and reality was an integral part of themselves.

The Vilna Gaon said that the events immediately pre-ceding the Exodus drew the Israelites' hidden spirituality to the surface. These spiritual effects were forever embodied in the mitzvot of mezuzah, tallit, and tefillin. Just as the Ten Plagues drew out the Jews' yearnings for God during the Exodus, these mitzvot also continually draw out and "re-deem" our deepest spiritual yearnings.

The *Sefer HaChinuch* gives reasons for the Torah's com-mandments (to the extent that we can fathom them). It says that wearing tefillin helps preserve and nourish our spiritu-ality in a materialistic world whose allures are constantly vying for our attention.[21]

Tefillin, then, confer a holiness that protects our eyes and heart so that we can see and love God, and keep us from being drawn to worldly temptations. They also help us dedicate our thoughts to the Almighty, as we need to do.

Tefillin and tzitzit are both defenses against sin. Just as soldiers take arms when they go into battle, Jewish men don these spiritual weapons as they prepare to battle the evil inclination every day. In this sense, tefillin and tzitzit are part of a Jewish man's uniform.

## The "Beautiful Woman"

These ideas are expressed more fully in the Torah's discussion of a Jewish soldier who falls in love with a beautiful Gentile woman on the battlefield.[22] If he wants to marry her, she must remove her ornaments for a month and mourn her family and nation because she must sever ties with them. If the soldier still loves her after watching her grieve so long without her wearing makeup or attractive clothes, she can begin the process of converting, and he can marry her.

The Torah permitted this because Jewish soldiers in biblical times were extremely spiritually developed. Men who weren't were disqualified from fighting in a war. Thus, men who had married that year, who had just built a home, or who had recently cultivated a new farm stayed behind. The pain of leaving a new wife, house, or farm was considered so great that it wasn't fair to make these men go to battle. These men stayed home, as did anyone who was afraid.

Jewish men were only afraid to fight if they had sinned, but even a minor moral or spiritual blemish was a reason for disqualification. Thus, the few soldiers who waged war possessed exceptional moral qualities. They knew that God was responsible for their victory, and it was not due to their military strength or prowess.[23] Therefore, they wore tefillin when they went into battle.

When the men tied the tefillin onto their arms, they recited a blessing thanking God for the opportunity to perform this mitzvah. This blessing also included the subsequent mitzvah of placing tefillin on the head. Men were not supposed to speak between wrapping tefillin around the arm and placing them on the head since one blessing applied to both. A man who did speak was required to say two additional blessings when he put on his head-tefillin and was disqualified from fighting.[24] Such a deed symbolized that the man's intellect, or belief and commitment to God (represented by the head-tefillin), was disconnected from his feelings (represented by the arm-tefillin that rest against the heart).

This was the magnitude of sin that disqualified potential soldiers from going to battle. Imagine having such a spiritually great army today!

How, then, could soldiers of this caliber have been attracted to Gentile women? One explanation is that many Jewish souls are held captive among the Gentile nations, and a Gentile woman who captivated such a soldier probably had such a soul.

Another explanation views the "captive woman" as a metaphor for our soul. The physical and sensual allures around us make us forget how beautiful our soul is, and leading superficial lives obscures our inner beauty. We can only reconnect with our soul by distancing ourselves from secular "adornments" and severing ties with the unholy people and pursuits with which we associate.

Our soul's true beauty can only express itself if we replace the distractions of this world with the adornment of tefillin and what they represent.

## God's Tefillin

The Talmud asks, "How do we know that the Holy One, blessed is He, puts on tefillin?"[25] It answers with a Scriptural verse, "God swore by His right hand [the Torah] and by the power of His arm (*uzo*)."[26] The Talmud says that whenever the word *uzo* is used, it refers to tefillin. It adds that tefillin are a source of strength for the Jews, as the Torah says, "And all of the peoples of the earth will see that the name of the Lord is called upon you, and they will be afraid of you."[27] The Talmud concludes that this refers to Gentiles seeing Jews wearing head-tefillin.

"What is written in the tefillin of the Master of the World?" the Talmud asks. It answers, "And who is like my people Israel, one nation on the earth?"[28] It adds, "The Holy One, Blessed is He, said to the Jews: You have made me a unique entity [the object of your love] in the world [by saying, 'Hear, Israel, the Lord is our God, the Lord is One'], and I will make you a unique entity [recipient of My love] in the world."[29]

God does not actually wear tefillin, but when Jews dedicate their hearts and souls to Him by wearing tefillin, He responds by extending His special providence and love to us. The Talmud underscores this idea by recounting stories where Jews were miraculously saved because they wore tefillin in the presence of their enemies.

Jews are the Almighty's "head-tefillin" in the sense that we are the central focus of Creation. We are in the forefront of His "mind" because His ultimate purpose for creating the world is bound up with us.

A Jew who wears tefillin unites the physical and spiritual worlds instead of succumbing to materialistic urges in a way that denies God's presence. Directing our eyes and heart only to God integrates holiness with the mundane aspects of life.

When we do this, the Almighty exclaims, "How great are

the Jews for unifying the physical and spiritual worlds." He then blesses us with His "eyes" and "heart." This exposes the "knot of God's head-tefillin."

This concept requires elucidation: The Torah says that Moses asked the Almighty to reveal the secret of His behavior toward man by requesting, "Please show me Your glory."[30] Moses wanted to understand why the righteous suffer and the wicked prosper, and to see the ultimate purpose underlying God's ways.

God replied, "Stand in the rock and I will pass by, but you won't be able to see My face because man can't see My essence and live. You can only see My back."[31] The Talmud says that the Almighty then showed Moses the knot on the back of His head-tefillin.[32]

Saying that God would not show Moses His "face," only the knot of His head-tefillin, means that mortals cannot understand the justice of divine ways in this world. God's behavior seems unjust because we have limited perceptions here. Part of our challenge is being asked to serve God while we cannot see the whole picture of life (God's face). When the present is behind us (God's back) in the Messianic era, all of the loose ends of our personal history, as well as the history of the world, will tie together.

Tefillin are tied with black straps, and the parchments are hidden in black boxes to convey the idea that God's purposes are dark and hidden. They can only be discovered once the dark barriers are penetrated.[33]

God's tefillin knot represents how His ways all underlie one central purpose. The straps extend down from the head-tefillin to the right and left sides. The right side represents God's ways of manifesting Himself with love, and the left side symbolizes His manifestation through strength and punishment. These are both means by which He brings the world to its intended goals. The straps hang down to represent God's guidance of the forces of history to their end point, always tied to the Jews' destiny (the knot on top). The knots are tied in the back because we can only understand the Almighty's ways once they are behind us, not when we are staring them in the face.

Insofar as the knot of God's tefillin represents His ties to His people, His "hand-tefillin" symbolize that the Jews' destiny is bound to everything that He does. His "hand" is an anthropomorphic way of referring to His actions. His purpose (head-tefillin) and actions (hand-tefillin) always relate to us as He guides history and supervises each Jew's individual destiny. The knot represents the place where Jews connect to Him as they find and reveal Him hiding behind the world's materialism.

### Notes

1. Deuteronomy 6:8, 9.

2. *Sefer HaChinuch*, mitzvah 421.

3. Aryeh Kaplan, *Tefillin* (New York: National Conference of Synagogue Youth, 1975), 52. The word for forbidden, *"assur,"* means bound.

4. Ibid., 48.

5. It is wrapped three times, symbolizing permanence.

6. Hosea 2:21, 22.

7. *Menachot* 34b.

8. If extenuating circumstances have caused only hand- or head-tefillin to be available, one should wear what he has. He will

at least fulfill some of the commandments pertaining to wearing tefillin that way.

9. *Menachot* 36a. Hand-tefillin are put on before head-tefillin because the Torah mentions the former first.

10. This parallels the four stages through which the world was brought into existence (the worlds of *atzilut, briah, yetzirah,* and *asiah*) and the one goal that they all serve.

11. *Menachot* 36b. A left-handed man puts them on his right bicep because the commandment is to put them on the weaker arm.

12. The necessity of having a clean body requires not wearing tefillin while passing flatus, or while having excrement on one's body.

13. *Menachot* 36b. The original commandment allowed men to wear tefillin at night. Today, if a man wore tefillin while it was still day, he may continue wearing them after nightfall.

14. Ibid. 44a.

15. Deuteronomy 6:8.

16. Exodus 31:13, 17.

17. *Menachot* 36b.

18. *Avnei Nezer:* see the laws of Shabbat at the beginning of the book.

19. Technically, a woman is allowed to wear tzitzit, provided they were made for her and not for a man. She must wear them only privately, as opposed to wearing them as a statement that she is proving her "equality" with men. Although women are permitted to wear tzitzit, few observant women have ever done so.

20. Aryeh Kaplan, *Tefillin,* 56, 57.

21. *Sefer HaChinuch,* mitzvah 421.

22. Deuteronomy 21:10–13.

23. Sadly, many modern Israeli soldiers and officers believe that their military skills, not divine providence, bring miraculous salvation. This is exactly the opposite of what Jewish soldiers believed for thousands of years.

24. *Menachot* 36a.

25. *Berachot* 6a.

26. Isaiah 62:8.

27. Deuteronomy 33:2.

28. I Chronicles 17:21. The verse continues, "...whom God went to redeem for Himself for a people, to make Himself a Name by great and tremendous things."

29. *Berachot* 6a.

30. Exodus 33:13.

31. Ibid. 33:19, 20.

32. *Berachot* 7a.

33. Aryeh Kaplan, *Tefillin*, 37, 38.

# 10

# The Second Paragraph of the Shema

The second paragraph of the Shema begins:

And it shall be, if you listen carefully to My mitzvot that I command you today, to love the Lord your God and to serve Him with all of your heart and with all of your soul, then I will give the rain for your land in its proper time, the early [which initially prepare the earth for growth] and the late rains [which allow the budding fruits to grow to maturity], and you will gather in your grain, your wine, and your oil. And I will give grass in your fields for your cattle, and you will eat and be satisfied. [1]

This paragraph of the Shema is known as "accepting the yoke of mitzvot." Once we accept God's authority as King, we want to know what He asks of us so that we can do it.

We accept God's government and acknowledge that He is our King because we must feel the importance of that relationship in order to perform our spiritual responsibilities properly. Otherwise, we will live as if the world's distractions

— such as work, physical pleasures, material possessions, honor, and prestige — are what make life worthwhile, and see God's will as less important. Accepting the primacy of a relationship with Him keeps us from treating mitzvot like items on a list that we try to dispose of while living our "real" lives.

Loving God and doing what He asks of us are interrelated. The Shema says that if we observe all of the mitzvot, we will reach the ultimate goal of loving God, but we cannot truly love Him without doing His commandments. This is because we live in a world where actions count, and we grow to love only as a result of actions. Thinking or emoting about the Almighty doesn't get us to really love Him. We must listen to the mitzvot, then do them, to achieve that goal.

The first paragraph of the Shema commands us to love God. The second paragraph says that once we love Him, we must concretize and demonstrate our feelings by accepting the yoke of His commandments. We show the depth of our loving feelings toward people by translating them into actions, and we do the same with the Almighty.

If a man tells a woman, "I love you dearly," but refuses to do anything for her, his love means little. True love leads to action. If actions do not follow, the love is questionable, at best.

This is why we concretize pledging allegiance to our Ruler's government in the first portion of the Shema by accepting His dictates in the second portion. We state what we are prepared to do and not do based on our love for Him.

One outgrowth of developing a strong relationship with God is that it gives us the religious strength to deal with obstacles and crises. Observing mitzvot without developing an overriding faith in, and closeness to, our Maker gives us little spiritual reserve with which to meet the predicaments and tribulations of life. When Judaism is the cornerstone of life, tragedies and losses don't shatter us.

People who live Judaism by rote often feel angry at God when disaster strikes. They contend, "I'm a good person. I do things for God, so why did He let such a terrible thing happen to me?" Without a deep relationship with the Almighty, there is no spiritual connection to fall back on when He acts in ways that defy their logic.

God challenges us by our successes, as well as by our failures and tragedies. Our life task is to develop a relationship with Him no matter what happens. That gives us a foundation and springboard for responding to any situation. When Judaism is our focus and everything serves our relationship with our Creator, we can always draw from the strength of having one main focus. We can't necessarily do that when we scatter our energies in many different directions.

Unfortunately, many people avoid facing God more than is absolutely necessary. They work a lot, then use their leisure time to relax and escape instead of making time to learn Torah, do charitable deeds, and/or work on their character traits. They compartmentalize their lives into times they serve God and times they do for themselves.

Everyone can find excuses to avoid drawing God into their lives, but people who see Judaism as their center find ways to overcome these barriers.

God didn't give us mitzvot in order to boss us around. Mitzvot are His way of saying that He wants us constantly to attach ourselves to Him so that we can feel His loving presence. This is why the word "mitzvah" comes from the Hebrew root *tzav*, which means attachment. Mitzvot are our vehicles for fulfilling our purpose in life, which is to attach ourselves closely to our Source.

Just as business people make sure to complete important work tasks every day, we should be careful to do God's tasks in a timely way. We can do this by studying Torah every day, making time for it regardless of how many other interests and desires beckon.

Accepting the centrality of a relationship with God before we do mitzvot shows Him where our hearts are. He doesn't want us to churn out mitzvot unemotionally and mindlessly, like a factory assembly line turns out machine parts. Nor does He want us to feel that we can be free of Him for the rest of the day as soon as we finish our daily obligations.

Centering ourselves on a relationship with God leads to our doing mitzvot in a way that expresses and overflows from a loving relationship with our Creator. Once we love the One who gave us commandments, we will want to do what He desires, and do it with a sense of attachment.

That is why the first paragraph of the Shema tells us to love God and serve Him with all of our resources. It reminds us to relate to Him constantly and make Him our life's focus. The second paragraph then expresses how accepting mitzvot logically results from a proper relationship with Him.[2]

## The First and Second Paragraphs of the Shema

The first and second paragraphs of the Shema contain many similar phrases, yet are not identical. The first paragraph says, "And you shall love the Lord your God with all of your heart, and with all of your soul, and with all of your resources (*me'odecha*)."[3] The second paragraph says, "And it shall be, if you listen carefully to My mitzvot that I command you today, to love the Lord your God and to serve Him with all of your heart and with all of your soul...."[4] Loving God with our money is conspicuously absent.

The first paragraph says, "And these words that I command you today should be on your heart. And you should teach them to your children, and speak of them when you sit in your house, and when you go on the way, and when you lie down, and when you rise up. And you should bind them as a sign on your hand and they shall be tefillin (phylacteries) between your eyes. And write them on the doorposts of your house and in your gates."[5] By contrast, the second paragraph says, "And you should put these words on your hearts and on your souls, and bind them as a sign on your hand, and they should be tefillin (phylacteries) between your eyes. And you should teach them to your children, and speak of them when you sit in your house, and when you go on the way, and when you lie down, and when you rise up. And write them on the doorposts of your house and in your gates."[6] The first paragraph tells us to put God's words on our hearts only, then to teach them to our children. The second paragraph says to put them on our hearts *and souls,* and to wear them as tefillin.

The first paragraph of the Shema requires us to internalize a personal commitment to God in every aspect of our lives, then transmit it to our children. Doing this "when you sit in your house and when you go on the way" means that we must do this not only when living a Torah lifestyle makes sense, but also when our faith is shaky, or the truth is not so clear. "When you lie down and when you rise up" alludes to this idea. There are times when we feel defeated by life ("lying down"), and we wonder if living a Torah way of life is worthwhile. We must "rise up" even when our belief is not so strong, including times when life is difficult.

Once we are religiously committed, we can, and must, transmit those beliefs in a meaningful way to our children. If we are conflicted about Judaism, we can't really teach it to others. Also, without having a relationship with Him, the rituals are rote and empty. The first paragraph of the Shema says that once we clarify our inner commitment, we must manifest it through outward signs, such as by wearing tefillin and putting a mezuzah on our doorposts.

It is also noteworthy that the first paragraph of the Shema is in singular form, and speaks to Jews as individuals. The second paragraph is in the plural. It tells us collectively to first do the rituals, then teach our children, then speak about God at various times.

We can commit ourselves either totally or partially to serving God. Individuals who do this totally are rare. Some of these people learn Torah all day and have no interest in material prosperity. Maimonides said that it is normally forbidden for a Jew to learn Torah and allow others to support him financially. Yet someone who is totally immersed in Torah study as a way of life may do this if he serves God "with all of his resources." He replaces his interest in material things with total dedication to the Almighty.

Most people have physical and spiritual needs. Rabbi Shimon bar Yochai lived in a cave for fourteen years, ate only carob from a nearby tree, and learned Torah with his son all that time. (He was hiding from Roman authorities who wanted to kill him.) He had no interest in physical pleasures and involvements. People like him don't care to be rewarded by material prosperity nor do they feel punished when physical things are taken away. This is the type of person whom the first paragraph of the Shema addresses. It is worded in singular form because such individuals are so unusual.

The second paragraph of the Shema is worded in plural form because it addresses most Jews. It doesn't say that we should serve God with "all of your resources" because we are not able to relinquish our desire for material comforts and pleasures. Instead, it warns us not to make materialistic pursuits into idols, and to keep them in their proper perspective.

The first paragraph tells the singular Jew to transfer his commitment to God to his children, then to display it outwardly. The second paragraph reverses this order. It tells the majority of us that we first need to deepen our commitment by reinforcing it with exterior signs such as mezuzah and tefillin, and then we will be able to transfer our commitment to our children.

Maimonides explained in the *Guide for the Perplexed* that the purpose of positive Torah commandments (the "thou shalts") is to help us deepen important ideas or feelings. If we don't express our thoughts or emotions through actions, they will disappear. Actions are a form of "packaging" that one generation can transmit to the next. Concrete actions remind us of important ideas, even when the original message seems to be forgotten. Doing positive commandments guarantees that we will transfer spiritual and moral messages, even when we don't understand them. This is why the second paragraph of the Shema tells most Jews first to put on tefillin, then to teach Judaism to their children.

The singular Jew who understands the deeper meanings of

Judaism can transmit relevant spiritual ideas directly. He is told to teach his children, then put on tefillin. Tefillin help reinforce his messages to his children, who may not be on his level.

## Hearing the Mitzvot

The first verse of the Shema's second section literally says, "If you listen, you will listen."[7] This can be interpreted as meaning that we should carefully and continually listen.

A deeper interpretation says that if we listen to the Almighty's mitzvot, we will later hear even more than we heard initially. We approach mitzvot at one level, but we can hear a lot more after actually doing them.

For example, many secular Jews find the detailed laws of observant Judaism archaic, illogical, or unnecessary, and are very critical of Torah Judaism. But when these critics actually try observing the Sabbath, holidays, family  holiness laws, and the like, they understand their beauty and importance in ways they couldn't before.

Paying attention to, and doing, the mitzvot is a developmental process, not an all-or-nothing experience. There are many shades of observance in between total observance and total neglect of mitzvot. Observance alone does not mean that we have reached the pinnacle of religiosity. Fulfilling our obligations is only the beginning of hearing what mitzvot are all about.

For example, we can mindlessly recite a blessing before we eat bread. That is better than not even giving lip service to the Almighty for His gift of food to us. Alternatively, we can say the blessing with a cognizance of what we are receiving, and from Whom. An even higher level of performing the same mitzvah is to make the blessing with the proper awareness of what we are saying and what we are receiving, with the intention that the food nourish us so that we can continue to serve God.

God's commandments were not meant to be ends in themselves, but means to a progressively deeper appreciation of the Being who commanded us. As we appreciate mitzvot more and more, so grows our appreciation for their Giver. This is especially true with respect to learning Torah.

## Today's Commandments

The Shema says, "And it shall be, if you listen carefully to My mitzvot that I command you *today*."[8] Inasmuch as God gave the Torah thousands of years ago, this verse means that we should always feel that mitzvot were given to us for the first time today.[9] When we yearn for something, we feel exhilarated when we finally get it. We should feel equally excited each time we have an opportunity to do a mitzvah. Since our excitement with new things tends to wane after a few moments or days, the Torah tells us always to do mitzvot as if we just got them.

Many Jews feel enormously excited as they become more and more observant. Every mitzvah feels thrilling, each opportunity to grow closer to God feels precious. Every Jew should have these feelings. No matter how many times we observe various mitzvot, we should put ourselves in a mindset of doing them with a sense of novelty and zeal.

The first section of the Shema said, "And these words that I command you *today* should be on your heart...."[10] Why is this idea repeated in the second paragraph, "And you should put these words on your hearts and on your souls..."?[11]

One reason is because novelty has two aspects: The first portion of the Shema applies to our decision to accept God's government every day. Rather than making this decision once when we are especially inspired, we must elect anew every morning to be the Almighty's servants and rededicate ourselves to Him.

The second portion of the Shema states our obligation to observe mitzvot. The second aspect of novelty applies to how we do things on a daily basis. The second portion of the Shema says that if we consistently do mitzvot and learn Torah, they will continually infuse us with new understandings and appreciation of what we do and learn.

Torah is not a legal body of knowledge that has something to teach only once. It always has new insights to offer, and we are required to study it so that we will reap these treasures.

These ideas lead to the question of why so many Jews only observe Judaism by rote if the Shema promises that learning Torah and doing mitzvot will always make them seem new. The answer is that people who do mitzvot to placate their conscience or social group, or in order to get rewards, do not develop a sense of excitement and freshness about Judaism. We must do mitzvot as a way of attaching ourselves to God or doing mitzvot won't have a constant dimension of novelty. Mitzvot are full of treasures, but their constant freshness depends upon our making them our core.

## Service of the Heart

The Shema's second section tells us to serve God with our entire heart and soul.[12] "Service of the heart" is prayer.[13] This section of the Shema specifically tells us to worship the

One Above by praying, in addition to observing all of His other commandments.

## Reaping God's Blessing

The Shema's second paragraph also tells us that if we do mitzvot, we will get an agricultural blessing and material satisfaction. Rashi said that this section means that if we do our part to serve God, He will do His part to help us live.[14] We can never guarantee what nature will provide, but the Almighty can because He controls it. We can only control how much of an effort we make to develop spiritually. We can't determine what will happen in most parts of our lives. The Talmud expresses this by saying, "Everything is in the hands of Heaven, except for reverence of Heaven."[15]

Most people spend lots of time and energy trying to master things that they can't control. The sooner we realize that we can only be real masters of our spiritual development, the better off we will be.

Living in an age of scientific and technological advances, we often think that we can accomplish our goals without God, but we can't. The Shema reminds us that we should try to control what is in our power, and not attempt to master what is solely up to the Almighty. If we do our best to rectify ourselves, God will provide what we need materially to continue serving Him.[16]

The Shema says, "And you will gather in your grain, your wine, and your oil."[17] The word "gather" is used because crops may grow well for a long time, then die at the last moment due to a drought, cold wave, blight, or attack by insects. They could also be seized by bandits or by our enemies. The Shema assures us that if we keep the mitzvot, we will harvest our crops, not only grow them.[18]

"And you will eat and be satisfied."[19] Food can be qualitatively or quantitatively satisfying. This verse does not mean that we will feel "stuffed" after eating a large quantity of food, but that we will feel satisfied and happy with whatever we eat.[20] This is more of a spiritual blessing than a physical one because we can eat less than usual, yet feel more satisfied than if we had eaten more. This is what happened when the first Temple stood. Every Sabbath the showbread was distributed to the officiating priests. Even though each received only an olive-sized morsel, eating it felt as satisfying as eating an entire meal. Satisfaction comes from our spiritual sensitivity and awareness of the Source of our food, not from the quantity we eat. When food is blessed within us, we feel nurtured by it.

## Getting Rewards

We are not rewarded in this world for our spiritual accomplishments. This is because nothing in this physical world can adequately recompense us for any mitzvah that we do. Since every mitzvah is a spiritual creation with eternal effects, nothing physical can be an adequate reward for it. Even if we could revel in *all* of this world's pleasures, it would not reward us appropriately for the simplest of mitzvot.

How, then, can the Shema promise us rain, crops, and physical satisfaction for observing the mitzvot?

One answer is that the rewards promised us in the Shema are not our primary rewards. They are simply "fringe benefits" of doing mitzvot.[21] Our ultimate rewards await us in the afterlife. God, in His goodness, provides whatever we need physically so that we can devote ourselves maximally to doing mitzvot. The more we use His world as He intended, the easier He makes it for us to continue doing so.

God designed the world always to be at our beck and call if we use it to serve Him. We are supposed to view this world as a corridor into a palace (the afterlife), and use our time here to reach that higher place. As long as we use this world as a means to an end, not an end in itself, God will insure that the world will foster our spiritual growth.

## The Land of Israel

The Torah contrasts the land of Israel with the land of Egypt before it presents the second section of the Shema: "The land that you are coming into to inherit is not like the land of Egypt that you left, where you sowed your seed and watered it by foot, like a verdant garden. The land that you are crossing over to possess is a land of hills and valleys. It drinks water from heavenly rain. (The land of Israel) is a land that God is constantly concerned about, and the eyes of the Lord your God are constantly upon it, from the beginning of the year to the end of the year."[22]

The Torah highlights the fact that people who live in Egypt can be more disconnected from God than can those who live in Israel. The Egyptians were actually cursed by their bountiful circumstances because they could believe that their crops grew independently of divine providence. They thought that the Nile and human efforts made them agriculturally successful. As long as water went where it was needed, and they could be sure that it did, their crops grew.

Paradoxically, Jews in Israel could not make crops grow merely by following the laws of nature. That was a blessing because it made them depend on God for their sustenance.

Since the land of Israel got its water from rain, not from a central river or reservoir, Jews could not make crops grow by relying on their efforts alone. When there was a shortage of rain, Jews had to address their relationship with God.

People often think that the most blessed situation is to have everything they want without challenge or struggle. Actually, we are cursed when our life circumstances don't encourage us to come closer to God. We prefer to rely on our efforts to ensure success and "make it" on our own, but that lets us live in a godless world.

This idea was expressed in the biblical story about the Garden of Eden. After the serpent convinced the man and woman to sin, God cursed the serpent to eat dust. We might think that this was a blessing since dust is everywhere. The serpent would never be hungry, no matter where he was. Yet it was a curse because he never connected his abundant food supply to the Creator who gave it, nor did he ever grow close to His Creator by virtue of what he received.

This idea was expressed in a parable of a king who gave his son an allowance.[23] When he gave his son money in one lump sum every year, he only saw his son once a year. When he gave it to him every day, the father saw his child every day.

God designed the land of Israel to encourage Jews to be close to Him and develop spiritually. To this end, the Torah says that God will give the land exactly what it needs, with neither shortages or surpluses. We expect no shortages to be a blessing, but how can a lack of surpluses be a blessing?

The Baal Akeidah said that both shortages and surpluses distract people from God. When we lack basic needs, we worry about how to survive. When we have plenty, we obsess about how much more we can make, or what we might lose. Thus, having either too much or too little can distract us from being totally dedicated to God. That is why having no shortages or surpluses in the land of Israel is so good. It facilitates having a relationship with the Almighty.[24]

While divine providence extends over the entire world, God's "primary focus" is His decisions about what happens in the land of Israel. What happens to the rest of the world follows from what happens there.

The Torah says that the land of Israel was designed to enhance our contact with our Creator. It is a country unlike any other, whose make-up encourages its inhabitants' spiritual growth. One can feel the divine Presence more readily there than anywhere else in the world.

That is why so many of the Torah's commandments are directly tied to the Holy Land. They include the requirement to tithe fruits, to give produce to the poor and to the priests, to let the land lie fallow during the Sabbatical years, and so on. These commandments are known as "mitzvot that depend upon living in the land of Israel," and they only apply there. Because God's providence is most heightened there, we need to be especially observant in His "backyard." We have more mitzvot to do there because we have a greater responsibility to live as Jews in Israel than anywhere else.

The Vilna Gaon told his children to be extraordinarily careful about how they performed mitzvot in the Holy Land. He termed Israel "the courtyard of the King." A Jew who acts improperly there "makes a mess in the King's courtyard."

Obviously, many people have the wrong attitude about Israel. The Almighty did not give us the land as an eternal inheritance so that we would prize its discotheques, Club Meds, bars, rock concerts, and soccer stars. Many Israelis think that as long as they live in Israel, they don't need to observe the Torah, and they claim that the mitzvah of inhabiting the land is in lieu of observing all other mitzvot.

Nothing could be further from the truth. The land's holiness requires our impeccable performance of mitzvot so that we can live in harmony with it. We must even eat produce and harvest our crops in Israel with a consciousness of God. As long as we do that, the Shema promises that the land of Israel will always provide for our material, as well as spiritual, needs.

The Shema tells us that if we use Israel simply as a place to live, and neglect mitzvot there, God will take away our land. He did this when we were exiled by the Babylonians and by the Romans. Israel only stays in our hands if we use it to come closer to God. The Torah and history both teach us that our right to the land of Israel will be contested, or lost altogether, if we don't behave as if the land is a tool for spiritual growth.

A midrash says that the Jewish people's spiritual merits guaranteed winning wars fought to protect the land of Israel. It was even said that the merit of saying the Shema sufficed to bring victory. This was because anyone who said the Shema with proper devotion and concentration viewed the land of Israel in its proper spiritual perspective, and lived accordingly. Such people then gained the right to remain there.

## Remembering God

After promising the Jews material abundance as a nation if they observe the commandments, the Shema says, "Watch yourselves, lest your hearts seduce you, and you go astray and serve strange gods, and bow down to them."[25] This is a reminder to be careful not to forget God when we "eat and are satisfied," and things go well for us. The Torah predicts that people who are satisfied and affluent will rebel against their Creator more readily than those who are impoverished.[26]

The Torah foretold that the Jews would "get full and kick [rebel]."[27] The Talmud says, "The lion [within us] does not roar from a diet of barley, only from a diet of meat." This means that our negative inclinations convince us to want more and forget God when we have affluence, more than when we live spartanly.

The Shema warns us to be especially careful to remember where our riches come from. We should use the blessings we receive to serve the One who gave them, not to indulge ourselves.

When the Shema says, "lest your hearts seduce you, and you go astray..."[28] it means neglecting learning Torah.[29] Once we do that, we will end up worshiping other gods, and will also "bow down" to them. This means that we will totally compromise ourselves by pursuing idols.

This does not mean that we will necessarily worship actual idols. Rather, we will think that forces other than God are responsible for our security and well-being, and will put our faith in things such as technology and money.

"And the Lord will be angry with you."[30] When a Jew misuses what God gives as a vehicle for worshiping Him, He eventually takes it away. Saying that God gets "angry" is a way of expressing His reaction to our mischanneling His blessings. When we do that, we prevent Him from giving us the bounty that He so much wants to give.

The more blessing we have, the more potential we have for misusing it. The land of Israel has tremendous potential for blessing. When we actualize that blessing, it greatly enhances our spiritual growth. When we don't, we mischannel its intense potentials negatively.

The Shema warns that God will then "hold back the heavens and there will not be rain, and the earth will not give its produce, and you will quickly be lost from the good land that the Lord gives you."[31]

This is analogous to a king who sent his son to a party after telling him what not to eat or drink there. The son didn't listen to his father, and he ate and drank too much. He then vomited and dirtied all of the party guests, who took him by the hands and feet and threw him out![32]

The land of Israel is a place for us to rejoice with the Almighty. We are supposed to enjoy the land's material blessings only in that context, not as ends in themselves. Someone who simply indulges in pleasures for his own enjoyment sullies himself. God then says, so to speak, "I told you how to behave in the banquet hall so that you would come home clean." If we use the land of Israel as a place to wine and dine ourselves while ignoring God's Presence, He will take away the land's bounty (and sometimes the land itself) so that we can no longer misuse it for our personal pleasure.

"Put these words on your hearts and on your souls, and bind them as a sign on your hand, and they should be tefillin between your eyes."[33] This means that the Shema should be written on the parchment that is in the tefillin (phylacteries) of the arm, and in the tefillin of the head.

"And you should teach them to your children."[34] Teach

them the message of the second portion of the Shema, which reminds us that God gives rewards and punishments for, respectively, obeying and disobeying Him. We should not raise children believing that everything will go well for them if they do mitzvot, but neglect teaching them the consequences of not keeping the mitzvot. Parents must educate children about both facets of God, His giving and His justice, not only make Him appear as wonderful and all-giving in human terms. We do children a disservice by covering up the fact that our King is also a Judge who punishes.

"[And you should] speak of them."[35] Teach your children to discuss Torah.

"...When you sit in your house, and when you go on the way, and when you lie down, and when you rise up."[36] Wherever we are, we talk about goals that are important to us. If our goals are to learn Torah and to do mitzvot, it will be easy to say a lot about them at home, on the road, and everywhere else.

## Mezuzah

"And write them on the doorposts of your house and in your gates."[37]

The Talmud says any Jew who does not have kosher mezuzot placed on the doors of his or her house violates two commandments.[38]

Mezuzot are parchments on which a Jewish scribe has written the first two sections of the Shema. They are only fit for use if they were written according to Jewish law. Contrary to popular belief, the beautiful covers that are sold by Judaica and gift stores are completely unnecessary, and are strictly ornamental. It is the mezuzot parchments which are essential, and they currently cost $25–65 if they are made properly. The majority of mezuzot sold in the United States during the 1960's were mere pieces of paper with the Shema printed on them. Some even said "Made in Japan" on the back! Unfortunately, huge numbers of unscrupulous or unknowledgeable merchants still sell invalid mezuzot scrolls today to unsuspecting Jews. If a bookstore or Judaica shop tries to sell you a bargain mezuzah scroll for $20 or less, it is unlikely to be kosher. Instead, look for kosher mezuzot that come in sealed packages with a board of rabbis' certification that they are legitimate. Local Chabad-Lubavitch rabbis can usually procure kosher mezuzot at cost, and can help you determine if your current mezuzot are kosher. They can also check if there are mezuzot on all of the relevant doorposts in your house.

Mezuzot are put on the right side as you enter the room, on the lower half of the upper third of each doorway.[39] They must be put on the doorposts of one's home and place of business if Jews own or rent the premises. When the parchment is rolled up, God's name *Sha-dai* appears on the outside. Its letters (*shin, dalet,* and *yud*) are the acronym for the words *shomer daltot Yisrael,* meaning "God guards the doors of the Jews."

Some people kiss the mezuzot when they pass by, especially the mezuzah on the front door when they leave the house. This particular mezuzah reminds us that God is constantly watching and guarding us, whether we are at home or elsewhere.

The Talmud relates a beautiful story about Onkelos, the nephew of a Roman emperor.[40] It enraged the emperor that

Onkelos converted to Judaism, and the emperor wanted to arrest him. Since Onkelos lived in Israel at the time, the emperor sent a contingent of Roman soldiers to bring him back. When the soldiers found him, Onkelos quoted Jewish Scriptures to them, and they were so impressed by these ideas that they went through the process of converting to Judaism.

The emperor then sent a second contingent of soldiers to fetch the renegade. This time, however, he warned the soldiers not to speak to Onkelos. Just as the soldiers were about to take him away, Onkelos said, "Let me just say one thing.... In a normal procession, the chief officer does not carry the light in front of the people. A common torchlighter carries it for him. Yet the Holy One, blessed is He, carries the light before the entire Jewish people." His words convinced this contingent to convert, just as his words had convinced the first group of Romans.

Onkelos gave a magnificent message to this second group. Pagans believed that their gods were powerful people with human limitations, lusts, and passions, but who lived in a different realm than humans. The Romans were impressed that the Jewish God was omnipotent, with no emotional or physical needs. He created people in order to give to and take care of them, not in order to have them take care of Him. The idea that the Jewish God was all-powerful, and desired only to take care of His creations, so impressed the soldiers that they readily abandoned their belief in gods that were limited, human creations.

The emperor then sent a third group of soldiers to arrest Onkelos, and commanded them not to talk to him, nor he to them. As the soldiers led him away, he saw the mezuzah on the door frame and put his hand on it, saying, "Every mortal king dwells inside the building, and his servants guard him from the outside. But the servants of the Holy One, blessed is He, dwell inside, while He guards them from outside." That group also converted to Judaism.

The pagan religions and Christianity developed from an assumption that their followers couldn't relate to the loftiness of an invisible, transcendent God. Since the Jewish God was a deity beyond their comprehension, they diminished Him by giving Him human qualities. The mezuzah is a constant reminder that our God is all-powerful, has no limits, and His Presence fills all the earth. His divine providence is always monitoring what happens to us as He protects us, whether we are at home, on a journey, or at work.

## Notes

1. Deuteronomy 11:13–21.

2. *Berachot* 13a.

3. Deuteronomy 6:4, 5.

4. Ibid. 11:13.

5. Ibid. 6:6–9.

6. Ibid. 11:18–20.

7. Ibid. 11:13.

8. Ibid.

9. Rashi on Deuteronomy 11:13.

10. Deuteronomy 6:6.

11. Ibid. 11:18.

12. Ibid. 11:13.

13. Rashi on Deuteronomy 11:13.

14. Ibid. 11:14.

15. Although we choose whether or not to fear God and do His will, our success in spiritual matters still requires His assistance.

16. Rashi on Deuteronomy 11:14.

17. Deuteronomy 11:14.

18. Cf. Rashi on Deuteronomy 11:14.

19. Deuteronomy 11:15.

20. Rashi on Deuteronomy 11:15.

21. Maimonides says that these are not even rewards for doing mitzvot. If we do what we are supposed to do, we merit the Almighty's increased investment in our future performance. According to him, these "fringe benefits" are really a divine investment in our future.

22. Deuteronomy 11:10–12.

23. *Yoma* 76a.

24. The Torah says elsewhere, "You will take out old grain [from the storehouses] in order to make room for the new." Shem Mishmuel commented that the purpose of these surpluses was to have produce that the Jews would sell to the Gentiles. When non-Jews would come to buy food from us, we would simultaneously teach them about God and morality.

25. Deuteronomy 11:16.

26. Rashi on Deuteronomy 11:16.

27. Deuteronomy 32:15.

28. Ibid. 11:16.

29. Rashi on Deuteronomy 11:16.

30. Deuteronomy 11:17.

31. Ibid.

32. Rashi on Leviticus 18:28.

33. Deuteronomy 11:18.

34. Ibid. 11:19.

35. Ibid.

36. Ibid.

37. Ibid. 11:20.

38. *Menachot* 44a.

39. *Menachot* 31b–34a discusses the laws pertaining to mezuzot. Very small rooms, such as small closets, and bathrooms do not get mezuzot.

40. *Avodah Zarah* 11a.

# 11

# The Third Paragraph of the Shema

In the second part of the Shema, we accept responsibility for performing the Almighty's commandments. The third part of the Shema reminds us that He took us out of Egypt. The significance of the Exodus was not its historical effects, but rather the eternal spiritual effects that it gave us.

When God created the world, goodness and negativity were totally separate. He wanted us to use our free will to choose goodness while being challenged to do the opposite. When Adam sinned in the Garden of Eden, he caused good and negativity to become mixed together so that it was no longer entirely clear which was which.

In the course of history, people chose to do many negative things. They hurt others, worshiped idols, and were sexually immoral, among other things. Things got to a point where doing evil dominated people's lives, and became almost a way of life.

God had wanted people to be good. Had they followed that path, they would have been worthy of wearing spiritual "crowns" that reflected their greatness and embodiment of divinity.

Our forefather Abraham differed from his predecessors by rejecting their way of life and beliefs. He tried to reverse the world's egocentricism by giving of himself, acting kindly, and seeking God's Presence everywhere. But he was only an individual, and the Master of the World wanted a nation that would bring the world's people back to Him and to His system of morality.

The Almighty wanted the world's Abrahams to become a nation that would fight negativity so intently that they would rectify the world. This is why the Israelites had to be exiled to Egypt some 3,500 years ago. They went into spiritual darkness, then were purified from negativity by receiving the Torah. This resulted in the Jews becoming a nation for whom goodness was a dominant force. Had the exile and subsequent Exodus never happened, Jews would have stayed disparate individuals with the right ideals, but would not have formed a unified group.

The Jews' Exodus from Egypt after 210 years of slavery was a phenomenal event, but not primarily because they gained physical freedom. It was significant because God separated goodness from negativity at that time, and restored goodness to its dominant role in the world. Taking the Jews out of Egypt after moral chaos had ruled for more than 2,000 years showed the world's people that they had operated long enough with a mixture of truth and falsehood. It was time for goodness and truth to regain their rightful place.

As long as negativity was mixed with enough truth to "sell" it, people tended to "buy" negativity. For example, many religions have a grain of truth along with a lot of falsehood. People follow these faiths because they have a small amount of obvious truth.

God clearly showed us real truth during the Exodus and at the giving of the Torah. Unfortunately, few people are willing to follow it.

In Egypt, the Jews didn't have the strength to wear the spiritual "crowns of humanity" that God wanted people to wear. A "spiritual crown" is a metaphor for something that allows us to fully actualize our potentials. Our greatness and self-actualization come from climbing spiritual heights. God wanted us to express our humanity by marshalling all of our efforts to live spiritually in a physical world. The Jews in Egypt were too immersed in negativity to live this way. A spiritual "poison" pervaded their beings and prevented them from having spiritual clarity. They had to get rid of that by being slaves in Egypt, then being redeemed.

The Jews were like gold whose dross was removed via a long refining process. By the time they left Egypt, they were purified, and their negativity was largely removed. Their Egyptian captivity did not create goodness because Jews always had that inside them, but it was buried under so many layers of impurity that the latter had to be peeled away.

Towards the end of this refining process, the One Above sent extra spiritual energy here.[1] This drew out the last remnants of goodness and completely separated it from the vestiges of impurity.

When the Jews experienced God's Presence and miracles in the year prior to the Exodus, they were willing to throw away the negativity and confusion that had been their constant companions for 210 years. Those who left Egypt knew clearly that falsehood and evil had no place in their lives. Other Jews, however, wanted to stay slaves to the allures of negativity, and they died in Egypt.

When God releases a tremendous amount of His energy into this world, it draws out goodness while destroying those who can't relate to it. This is why evil people (such as the first-born Egyptians) were shattered by His revelation during the Ten Plagues. They couldn't contain such enormous goodness. The plagues were a series of disasters that progressively manifested more and more of the Almighty's greatness and holiness. It drew those people closer who could relate to it, while it destroyed those who could not relate to it.

This splitting of goodness and negativity raised people above the confusion that had ruled them almost since Creation. This gave us a completely different identity, the effects of which will last forever. The world can no longer go back to its previous state of confusion, nor can negativity predominate again.

The Exodus plays such a central role for us because that was when God restored goodness and truth to their proper places. People could once again wear their spiritual "crowns" and live with a proper sense of direction. It reinstated a clarity about what is right and wrong to the Jews individually, as well as nationally. This allowed our full potentials to emerge from captivity. That, in turn, enabled us, and the world, to return to the spiritual state that was always meant to be.

Had goodness not regained its original primacy, the world would have had no future. People would have stayed utterly confused forever, and would have continued to pursue non-spiritual directions. This is why so many mitzvot commemorate the Exodus. For example, when we sanctify the Sabbath or holidays over a cup of wine (kiddush), we mention that it commemorates the Exodus.

Since the Torah existed before people, its mitzvot are independent of historical events. Every mitzvah expresses God's will and has inherent value. This implies that had the Jews never been enslaved and freed, mitzvot commemorating the Exodus would still be necessary because the Exodus prevented the forces of good and evil from staying confused forever. Mitzvot are irrelevant if we don't know how to choose goodness over evil and falsehood.

The Exodus, then, represented God's reorganization of the world's spiritual forces. In gratitude for this gift, we observe mitzvot, and make goodness and spiritual purpose dominate our lives. Thus, mitzvot don't commemorate the historical fact of the Exodus; they celebrate the re-establishment of goodness' strength and its separation from negativity, which lets us know clearly how to live.

Because of the Exodus, Jews can never lose the ability to be good and refrain from doing bad. Since the Jewish nation was born when God split the forces of good and evil, our birthright gives us the ability to also separate these forces. When we perform mitzvot and study Torah, they always strengthen us so that we can make goodness dominate our lives.

## Three Types of People

The Maharal (a commentator on the Torah) says that there are three types of people: *chomer, tzurah hamutbaat bachomer,* and *tzurah nivdelet. Chomer* is a person whose entire existence is defined by materialism, and who totally identifies with it. He has no ability to relate to any kind of spirituality.

*Tzurah hamutbaat bachomer* is a person with some spiritual identity, but who can't break away from materialistic connections. Such people leap for the stars while their feet are mired in mud. Their spiritual identity is imprisoned in materialism. They have a more difficult challenge than *chomer* people because people who are all *chomer* eventually lose the vitality that comes from materialistic pleasure alone. When that happens, they sometimes search for an authentic spiritual life. But the *tzurah hamutbaat bachomer* relates to the materialistic world while building ideologies and cultures around it. Once people develop principles about the importance of materialism and physical pleasure, they are loathe to abandon them. They can't easily extricate themselves from these pursuits even when they want to do so.

The third type of person, *tzurah nivdelet*, is full of spiritual energy. The only relationship such a person has with the material world is to elevate it spiritually. Physical drives and pleasures have no control over such a person's spirituality. Goodness is so separate from negativity in them that goodness dominates all else. They can stay totally aloof from the seductions of negativity and materialism.

When the Jews left Egypt, they became *tzurot nivdelot*. From then on, Jews could live in the physical world while part of their souls remained unaffected by materialism. No matter what, part of us never loses its purity and is always detached from the physical world.

Every Jewish soul has a *pintele yid*, a spiritual pilot light that never goes out. That resulted from the splitting process that occurred during the Exodus. Our souls received eternal protection from the negative influences of the material world such that part of our spirituality remains untainted by any materialistic pursuits, and it can always be developed.

All goodness that has entered the world since the Exodus came because we became *tzurot nivdelot* — separated from the material influences on our souls. The Almighty requires us to remember that. Recalling and thanking Him for the Exodus every day when we say the Shema sensitizes us to the importance of, and reward for, committing ourselves entirely to goodness and Godly pursuits.

The more we refer to the Exodus, the more spiritual light we bring into the world, just as happened when the Jews left Egypt. We are constantly corrected and nurtured by the effects of the split that occurred at that time in history.

We never say the Shema because our Creator needs to hear it. We do it because it helps us clarify what is real and what is illusion. Doing this twice a day helps strengthen us and aids us in discerning how to live properly.

## The 248 Words

Not only are the Shema's themes and words important, but even its number of words conveys a spiritual message. When we say the Shema with a minyan (at least ten Jewish men), the reader repeats the last three words, "*Ad-noi Elokeichem Emmet,*" ("the Lord is our true God"). This phrase gives the Shema a total of 248 words. If we say the Shema without a minyan, we must add three words at the beginning, "*Kel Melech Ne'eman*" ("God is a true King"). This also constitutes a total of 248 words, since we don't repeat the last three words when there is no minyan.

Judaism considers people to have 248 limbs, each of which corresponds to the world's 248 major functions.[2] By using our 248 body parts correctly, we spiritually sustain and energize the world's 248 parallel parts. We are so integrally connected to the world that the human being is called an *olam katan* — a "microcosm of the world."

Our 248 body parts and the world's 248 functions always radiate with the light of God's unity. Saying the Shema's 248 words draws divine light into our bodies and into the world. This is so important that, when we pray alone, we must add additional words to the Shema to symbolize this.

## Notes

1. This is referred to as "strengthening His nurturing and giving of His light to the Jewish people."

2. There are also 248 positive mitzvot, each of which spiritually energizes a corresponding limb of the body.

# 12

# The Mitzvah of Fringes — Tzitzit

$B$eloved are Israel, for the Holy One, blessed is He, surrounded them with precepts: tefillin on their heads, tefillin on their arms, tzitzit on their clothes, and mezuzot on their doorposts."[1]

"Anyone who has tefillin on his head, tefillin on his arm, tzitzit on his clothes, and a mezuzah on his doorpost is absolutely secure against sinning."[2]

"And Abram said to the king of Sodom, '...I will not take a thread, nor a shoelace, nor anything that belongs to you....'[3] Because of this, the Almighty gave his children the mitzvah of wearing fringes (tzitzit)."[4]

The third paragraph of the Shema says:

> The Lord spoke to Moses, saying: Speak to the children of Israel, and tell them to make themselves fringes (tzitzit) on the corners of their garments for all their generations; and they should put a blue strand on the corner fringe. And you will have tzitzit, and you shall see them, and you will remember all of the Lord's commandments, and do them. And you shall not stray after your hearts and after your eyes, that you lust after,

so that you will remember and do all of My commandments, and be holy to your God. I am the Lord your God
who brought you out of the land of Egypt to be your God.
I am the Lord your God.[5]

Tzitzit are several white strands of wool bound together
with at least one blue strand, that are then attached to the
corners of a four-cornered garment.[6] The blue strand is
wrapped around the white strands seven times and is knotted. It is then wrapped around the white strands another
eight times and is knotted again. Ultimately, each set of
tzitzit has five knots around its eight threads.

Every Hebrew letter has a numerical value. The numerical value of all of the letters in the word tzitzit equal 600.
That, plus the five knots and eight threads, equals 613, the
total number of commandments in the Torah. Thus, looking
at the tzitzit reminds us to observe all 613 of God's laws.

There was once a fish called a *chilazon*, whose blood was
used to dye the strands blue. It was so rare that, in ancient
times, this fish only rose to the ocean's surface every seventy
years.[7] Since it is now unclear what species of fish this was,
we don't currently dye strands blue.[8] Instead, we observe
the mitzvah of tzitzit using only white strands. The original
ones, however, were both blue and white.

The Talmud says that the punishment for not performing the mitzvah of tzitzit involving the white strands is more
severe than for neglecting the part with the blue strands.[9]
God's command that we dye one strand blue is analogous
to a king who commanded two servants to make royal
emblems. One was told to make an emblem of gold, while
the other was told to make it out of clay. A month later, the
king summoned them, wishing to inspect the emblems,

only to discover that neither did as he was commanded. The king was angrier with the one who didn't make the clay emblem because clay is inexpensive and easy to procure. Since that subject had no excuse for neglecting the order, he was more accountable for his misdeed than the one who did not make the gold emblem.[10]

A man who did not even wear tzitzit of white strands is analogized to the servant who did not make the clay emblem. Someone who didn't wear tzitzit with the blue thread is like a servant who didn't make the gold emblem, since blue dye was rare, like gold. A Jew who neglects an easy mitzvah is more culpable than one who neglects a more difficult one.[11]

On a different level, though, this analogy teaches us about the two kinds of royal emblems that the different strands of the tzitzit exemplify: One is common, the other is more precious. The common emblem represents our body and physical existence, while the precious one represents our soul.

Our soul is our essence. Our body is merely a garment that allows the soul to exist in the physical world. Tzitzit are garments that remind us that our bodies are also garments. Our essential self is our soul within. Seeing the tzitzit at the ends of a garment remind us that physical life ends, which prompts us to think seriously about our life's purpose. Just as tzitzit extend beyond the ends of a garment, so should we think about what is beyond the end of our physical lives. Tzitzit, then, remind us of our mortality and the spiritual afterlife that our soul enters when life here is over.

The *Ethics of the Fathers* graphically illustrates this. It says that we must contemplate three things in order to live meaningfully: Where we came from, where we are going, and in front of Whom we will need to give an accounting. It says that we come from a foul drop; that we are going to a place of worms; and that we will need to give an accounting for our lives before the King of the universe.[12]

This reminds us not to aggrandize our bodies' importance into our life's focus. We must put our physical existence into proper perspective. A body that comes from nothing and eventually decomposes cannot be our primary identity, so we shouldn't view it as such. We should focus on our true identity, which is our soul and our spiritual accomplishments. The more we downplay our body's significance as other than a vehicle to elevate our soul and the world, the more we can appreciate our soul's centrality and pursue spirituality. The more we make our bodies ends in themselves, the less significant our souls seem.

Still, we can learn how to be godly by noticing our bodies' design, intricacy, and functions. Everything in the physical world teaches us something about its Creator and how He intended us to use His world, and our bodies are prime examples of this. For instance, our heads are higher than our bodies, which is not the case with many animals. This teaches us that our intellect (head) should rule our emotions, rather than our letting our feelings dictate how we act and being slaves to our drives. Our bodies have two ears and only one mouth so that we will listen more than we speak. Our mouths have lips and teeth in front of them so that we will carefully guard what goes in and out of them. Our ears and eyes have barriers that we can close to keep out information that we should not let in.

In other words, part of what our bodies teach us is that we should let our senses enjoy the physical world, but not indiscriminately. We are supposed to integrate the physical world with our spiritual selves. This means that rather than being ascetics, we sanctify and enjoy the food that we eat and drink, the fragrances that we smell, and even the physical intimacy that we share with our spouses.

Yet Jews sometimes fast, and we must abstain from marital relations on a regular basis. Obviously, such abstinence negates the physical world, so why do we do it? Because abstaining periodically allows us greater contact with our spirituality. Occasionally withdrawing from full enjoyment of the physical world helps us to refocus on our spiritual dimension. Developing our bodies' potentials for creating sanctity allows us to be God-like.

Observing the Sabbath also helps us periodically detach from the physical world. As we withdraw from our material involvements, we get in touch with our core, inner dimension. This keeps our spiritual "circuits" from getting overloaded with physical messages that mask our souls' importance. When we immerse ourselves in continual material creativity, it keeps spiritual messages from coming through.

The white of the tzitzit symbolizes the soul's physical garment — our body. The blue symbolizes the soul that comes from "under the (divine) Throne of Glory." The Talmud says that the blue of the tzitzit reminds us of the blue of the ocean. This, in turn, reminds us of the blue of the sky. This prompts us to reflect on the awesomeness of the universe and the God who created it.[13]

The "Throne of Glory" symbolizes the King of kings,[14] so that the blue of tzitzit motivates us to think about Him.

The soul is "God's emblem of gold." Just as gold is

precious, so is the soul God's precious emblem. But the soul cannot reach its maximal potential without using the body. Only by rectifying and elevating the body, the clay emblem, can the soul actualize itself. Our life's purpose is to identify primarily with our "gold" emblem and to integrate our physical self with our spiritual one.

This is why we are punished more for neglecting the white strands than for neglecting the blue ones. We must first see our bodies' true purpose (symbolized by the white strands) before we can truly appreciate our soul (symbolized by the blue strands).

Garments are coverings that we put on and take off. We change them frequently, yet we stay constant. If we believe that "clothes make the man" instead of being here only to serve us, we are in trouble. We have to know that our earthly garments (bodies) are mere coverings that were given to serve a permanent soul that will continue in a realm after our life here.

We are the King's servants in the parable. We must serve Him by making emblems for ourselves so that we can live meaningfully. This is why we make tzitzit. They remind us to de-emphasize the physical as an end in itself and use it to develop our spiritual essence.

The blue symbolizes that we are God's children whose souls belong to Him. They come from "under His Throne of Glory." Just as a child gets his parents' genes, so do we have God's spiritual characteristics in us. Our souls come from His essence.

Both our physical and spiritual sides help us relate to God. Our body teaches us what we should accomplish during our stay in this world, while our soul reminds us about the lineage that we have from our Father.

## The Power of Mitzvot

Every mitzvah draws spiritual light into the physical world. Looking at tzitzit helps us put our physical and spiritual selves in proper perspective. A man who wears tzitzit is better equipped to win the battle between his spirituality and his physical desires. They help him remember that his body is only a garment.

The Talmud relates a story about an infamous prostitute who was exceptionally beautiful, and whom men traveled long distances and paid exorbitant fees in order to patronize. A Jewish man heard about her, traveled many miles to see her, and paid a fortune for her services. Prior to having relations with her, he had to climb up a ladder to her bed. As he climbed, his tzitzit hit him in the face and brought him to his senses.

When she saw that he had suddenly lost interest in her, she said, "I will not leave you until you tell me what blemish you saw in me."

He replied, "I swear that I have never seen a woman as beautiful as you, but the Lord our God has commanded us to wear tzitzit. The Torah repeats in regard to this, 'I am the Lord your God.' This means that He is the One to punish us in the future and to give reward in the future. Now my tzitzit appeared as four witnesses testifying against me."

Not only did he leave without touching her, she was so impressed by his behavior that she converted to Judaism.[15] This story teaches us the power that tzitzit wield in strengthening us not to compromise our spiritual integrity for physical pleasure.

Mitzvot are not simply divine directives about what to do or not do. They are support systems that help us overcome our challenges and remind us of our true identities. God knows that we need help battling our physical drives, so He gave us mitzvot that nurture us to live up to our spiritual potentials. Wearing tzitzit on our clothes reminds us that our bodies are our souls' garments. Tzitzit also help us live up to that ideal.

Even though tzitzit can help protect us, they can't do it regardless of how we live. A man can't read pornographic magazines and think that tzitzit will protect him from untoward thoughts or inappropriate behavior. Mitzvot give some protection, but only in the context of our other actions.

## Following Our Eyes

The final portion of the Shema says that wearing tzitzit will prevent a man from following his heart and eyes so that he will not come to sexual immorality. The Hebrew word for such immorality is *"zenut,"* but *zenut* really means "straying." A Jew who is sexually immoral is straying from his true identity into a realm that does not belong to him. Looking at tzitzit reminds us, and strengthens us, not to make forays into places that we shouldn't go with our eyes and hearts. Our eyes see something appealing, our hearts start fantasizing about it, and then we want it.[16] Tzitzit interfere with the intensity of that process.

Rashi says that our bodies have two limbs that make us "travel." These are our eyes and our hearts.[17] We should only be drawn to the inner meanings of things, not be seduced by outward appearances. Even though we tend to notice what's on the outside, we should train ourselves to focus on the essence of things. That is a challenge that requires tremendous discipline.

Tzitzit help us see people's inner essences instead of being distracted by their physical beauty. We should direct our sight only to what God wants us to see, such as someone's inner beauty, not the contours of his or her flesh. Doing this automatically puts us more in touch with the Source of physical creation, and makes us less distracted by what is external.

We are vulnerable to, and most controlled by, things that attract us. The more we pay attention to physical appearances, the more they control us. When we see the spiritual essence behind the physical, and look to its purpose and Creator, we are only controlled by the One who put all material existence here.

Our forefather, Abraham, was childless for many years. He was a gifted astrologer who read his future in the stars, and he saw that he would never have children. According to the laws of nature, it was reasonable for him to have given up wanting descendants. But the Almighty told him to go outside and gaze above the stars. He then promised Abraham descendants who would be as numerous as the lights that he saw in the sky.[18]

As long as Abraham believed that he would not have a child through natural means, he could not. On the other hand, once he looked beyond nature to the One who created and controlled nature, he could supersede it. God can give anybody a child, and often does defy the laws of nature in this regard. But in order to do this, Abraham had to "go outside" his mindset that nature determined his fate. He had to look to the Source of nature for what he wanted.[19]

Abraham had Isaac when he was one hundred years old and Sarah was ninety. Obviously, her conception transcended nature. This was so the Jewish people's genesis would not be locked into nature. Our roots were drawn from a Source that is above natural limitations. Abraham had to work on himself not to put too much stock in physical and external appearances.

## The Eyes and Hearts

The Torah always has at least nine spaces between one portion and the next, except for the portions of "*Vayigash*" and "*Vayechi*" that appear in the book of Genesis. *Vayigash* discusses the Israelites' descent into Egypt, while *Vayechi* discusses Jacob's death, and only one space separates them. Rashi comments that the usual gap between portions is closed to indicate that the eyes and hearts of the Israelites were closed by the suffering the Egyptians caused them when Jacob died.[20]

We know that severe Egyptian oppression of the Israelites did not begin until Moses was born and the last of Jacob's sons passed away. That took place more than eighty years after Jacob died. Rashi's comment, then, refers to the Jews' spiritual oppression, not to their physical slavery.

We can understand this better with the help of an explanation by the Chatam Sofer. He said that we can primarily relate to God out of a sense of reverence and awe, or out of a feeling of love for Him. The former is called *yirah*, which also means "to see." If we would only see God as He truly is, we would immediately be filled with awe. When Jacob died, the Israelites' loss of a role model, who could be in awe of and deeply love the Almighty, made it hard for them to "see" God. Rashi expressed this by saying that the Israelites' eyes (fear of God) and hearts (love of God) closed when their forefather died.

The third paragraph of the Shema tells us not to stray after our hearts and our eyes. "Hearts" refers to false ideologies and idol-worship. The latter is rarely rooted in honest intellectual searching for truth. It comes from an attempt to rationalize and justify inappropriate behavior. Most of the time, we choose false ideologies because we listen to our hearts instead of to our minds.

Not following our eyes means that we should not let ourselves be enticed into immoral behavior. Idol-worship and sexual immorality were the Egyptians' two greatest vices, and historically these were major areas where Jews' eyes and hearts led them astray.

When our eyes see, and our hearts desire, spiritual garbage, we act on our impulses. That is why the Shema tells us to consecrate our eyes and hearts, not only our deeds, to serving God.

We tend to think that what we do is more important than what we think, but our behaviors are not born in a vacuum. They result from how we process what we see and feel. Since everything we do flows from our eyes and our hearts, we must be careful to protect them. Wherever they are spiritually, we are, too.

God, as it were, has eyes and a heart. He told King Solomon, "I have sanctified this house that you have built to make My Presence known there forever. My eyes and My heart will always be there."[21] God's "eyes" symbolize His interest in and concern for us. This is what we call divine providence. His "heart" refers to His love for us. By directing our eyes and hearts to Him, we "allow" Him to connect His eyes (divine providence) and His heart (love) to us.

All too often, we want to live as if God is not continually watching us, so that we can be free to do as we please. The pressure that we would feel always to live up to our souls' potential is so uncomfortable that most people live as if God closes His eyes to our misdeeds.

When the Jews' eyes and hearts closed after Jacob's death, they let themselves become attracted to the wrong things. God responded by distancing Himself from them. They then had difficulty seeing His closeness and feeling His love. They lost their sense of awe and love for Him, with disastrous consequences.

## *The Spies*

In the Torah, the third paragraph of the Shema follows an episode involving twelve Jewish spies.[22] These tribal leaders scouted out the land of Israel before the Israelites entered it. Ten of them said terrible things about the land to the Jewish people. For example, they said that it was impossible to conquer Israel or live there because it was inhabited by giants and mighty warriors.

While it was true that the Jews were weaker than the land's inhabitants, they still should not have despaired. The Israelites were not subject to the laws of nature during the Ten Plagues, nor when they left Egypt, nor during their travels in the desert. They lived with the Almighty constantly making miracles for them. For this reason alone, they should have trusted His promises to help them conquer the resident nations and settle in Israel. The Jews should have relied on the Almighty to do things His way, not tried to take control through natural means.

The third portion of the Shema follows the spy episode

because the spies were drawn to outward appearances. This part of the Shema tells us not to stray after our hearts and our eyes, which is what the spies did. The One who created all physical laws promised that generation, as well as us, that we can transcend nature if we only listen to Him. Tzitzit remind us of this lesson.

## *Seeing Reality, Not Illusion*

The Talmud tells about a woman who once threatened to harm Rabbi Chanina ben Dosa using witchcraft. He was unfazed, and assured her that she could not harm him using the powers of impurity.

Other rabbis asked Chanina ben Dosa why he was so sure that he wouldn't be harmed, inasmuch as God gave the forces of impurity the power to hurt people. Chanina ben Dosa replied that he firmly believed that God was the only ultimate force in the world. Unless He wills that someone be harmed, negative powers are totally ineffective against that person.

The witch tried her magic on him and nothing happened. He explained, "If I had believed in the external and apparent force of witchcraft, I would have been vulnerable to it. It could have controlled or hurt me. But since I fully believe that there is no force other than God, nothing happened."[23]

If we are taken by life's superficialities, we can live with many illusions. If, instead, we focus on why we are here and what the One Above expects of us, we won't fritter away our lives chasing wordly allures. The more we attach ourselves to the physical, the more it becomes our lifeblood and identity.

Spiritual goals elude us as long as we feed on sensual

gratifications. We convince ourselves that spirituality is too hard to attain, then settle into superficial lives. The more we commit ourselves to living superficially, the more we believe that ongoing spirituality is only for saints.

The Sfat Emmet said that no mitzvah is ever beyond our reach. Even if we previously sinned, or don't think much of ourselves, any service of God is really only out of reach if we are deluded by the world's trappings. Our negative inclination tells us that our potential growth is limited, and we believe it. But with our Creator's help, no mitzvah is beyond us. He gave us our ultimate life force, and that makes it possible for us to connect to any mitzvah. The more we do mitzvot, the more they fuel us and the entire world.

## A Thread and a Shoelace

In the Torah portion of *Lech Lecha*, King Nimrod started a war in an attempt to draw Abraham into battle and kill him for believing in God. During the war, Nimrod's army captured Lot, Abraham's nephew. Abraham entered the fray with a small army of his own and defeated Nimrod's side. Abraham released his nephew, then returned all of the booty and people that he and his men had captured from the kingdoms of Sodom and Gomorrah.

The king of Sodom told Abraham, "Give me the people who were imprisoned by the four kings, and keep the booty for yourself."[24]

Victors in any war keep what they take or conquer. Yet Abraham vowed to the king of Sodom, "I will not take a thread, nor a shoelace, nor anything that belongs to you. I don't want you to say, 'I made Abram rich.'"[25]

Rashi commented that Abraham wanted God to make

him rich, in fulfillment of a divine promise.[26] Had Abraham taken even the smallest item from the king of Sodom, the king would have harbored the mistaken belief that he, not God, had made Abraham rich.

On other occasions, Abraham accepted food from a priest named Malchizedek, and a gift of livestock and servants from Pharaoh.[27] This makes us wonder why he acted differently with the king of Sodom.

God never told Abraham that he would become rich in a miraculous way, so it would seem that there was nothing wrong with Abraham keeping the booty that he had acquired. Why, then, did he make sure that the king of Sodom would not be the Almighty's agent for fulfilling His promise?

The Talmud says that Abraham was rewarded for not taking even a thread from the king of Sodom by his descendants getting a mitzvah that involved threads. This mitzvah is tzitzit. The Almighty also rewarded Abraham for not taking a shoelace from the king of Sodom by giving Abraham's descendants the mitzvah of tefillin.[28]

When the *Shulchan Aruch* (Code of Jewish Law) tells us how to get dressed in the morning, it says that we should tie our left shoe before our right one. The word for tying a shoe is the same as that for tying tefillin (*likshor*), suggesting that the way we tie our shoes is related to the way we tie tefillin.

We will understand the importance of this better by digressing to the mitzvah of *chalitzah*. In biblical times, if a married man died without having children, his brother was supposed to marry his widow and have children with her. This was known as a levirate marriage, and it was done to perpetuate the name of the deceased. If the brother refused to marry the widow, he had to go through a ceremony called *chalitzah.* In this ceremony, the widow removed her brother-in-law's shoe,[29] while spectators said, "This is what is done to a man who refuses to uphold his brother's name."

As long as we live, our physical part (the body) can elevate our soul by doing God's commandments. When we die, our souls become passive because they can only grow as long as they are in a body. Having once been in this world, they desire to stay connected to it.

The essence of one's soul stays in contact with this physical world through one's children. When a levirate marriage caused a child to be born, it allowed part of a man's soul to stay connected to this world.

The Hebrew word for name, "*shem,*" consists of the letters *shin* and *mem*. This forms the root of the Hebrew word "*neshamah,*" which means "soul." This expresses the idea that one's name is at the core of one's soul. A name stays in this world after the rest of a person departs. That is why Ashkenazic Jews name babies after deceased relatives, and Sephardic Jews name them after the living. It keeps someone's name in this world.

When a person dies childless, his "name" suffers because it can't attach itself to this world. Part of the soul desperately wants to come back here, but it can't. Its agony was alleviated when the widow married a close male relative of her deceased husband, and they produced a child who received holy sparks from the deceased's soul. That allowed the deceased to have ongoing contact with the physical world.

Shoes are the garment that lets us stay in contact with the earth. Both shoes and bodies are garments, points of contact that allow our physical part to connect to the spiritual. A soul can only connect to this world if it has a "shoe" (body).[30]

Thus, a man who fathered children through a levirate marriage gave the soul of a deceased man a "name." A relative who refused to do this had his shoe removed in the *chalitzah* ceremony to symbolize that he had taken away a man's connection to this world.

Tefillin, the shoes of *chalitzah*, and tzitzit are all tied to symbolize their ability to connect our spiritual selves to the physical world. Tefillin connect our thoughts, emotions, and actions to the Almighty. Tzitzit are fringes that we wear on the ends of our clothes, which is where we contact our surroundings. The knots on tzitzit symbolize tying the spiritual and physical worlds together. When Abraham told the king of Sodom that he would not take "a thread" nor "a shoelace" from him, he indicated that he would not compromise his spiritual connection with the physical world.

While Abraham knew that everything he had was a result of divine providence, the king of Sodom did not believe that. Were Abraham to accept the slightest gift from this wicked king, the king would believe that he made Abraham rich. Abraham made sure that the king would not use Abraham's situation to reinforce his own warped ideology.

Jews like Abraham, who are in the public eye, must be especially careful not to desecrate God's Name and discredit Judaism. One talmudic rabbi even said that it would desecrate God's Name if he took merchandise from a store without paying for it, even though he would pay for it later.[31] Technically, he would not have done anything wrong, but if some people had misconstrued his actions to conclude that rabbis can act above the law, that would desecrate God's Name. In such situations, Jews must act "beyond the letter of the law."

Jews need always to wear symbolic tallit and tefillin, even when we don't wear them physically. Tallit and tefillin remind us to show our special spiritual qualities all of the time, whether we are talking to other people, sitting at home, working at our jobs, or doing business. We should always be conscious that everything we do affects our souls and reflects upon our relationship with God. These religious items symbolize the moral integrity with which we should always behave, especially towards others. We may not act in ways that desecrate God's Name. As God's special emissaries, we must also do our utmost not to act in ways that allow others to distort the truth. Tallit and tefillin remind us that we always wear God's uniform and must act in consonance with the lofty mission that our garments represent.

Abraham's unwillingness to take even a thread or a shoelace from the king of Sodom came from his sense that he always wore a tallit and tefillin. God rewarded him measure for measure by giving his descendants the merit of these two mitzvot.

## Summary

Tzitzit tell us not to focus on our garments (bodies) as ends in themselves and remind us to focus on our souls. When we discipline ourselves not to chase the "garments" of life, we have the strength to do spiritual things that seemed so difficult we didn't think we could do them. We interfere with our ability to elevate ourselves spiritually when we lock ourselves into the allures of the physical world. But we can defy natural law to the extent that we do not expect it to nurture us spiritually. The more we look to the Source of our souls, the more strength we find to do mitzvot.

Tzitzit are a Jewish man's uniform. They remind him, and those who see them, that our calling is to do mitzvot and transcend the physical world. If we take our "garments" seriously, we will use our bodies to do mitzvot and learn Torah, while simultaneously weaving spiritual "garments" that we will don in the World to Come.

## Implications for Human Relationships

Tzitzit teach us the importance of looking beyond superficialities to the essence of things. In an otherwise loving relationship, one person may be so hurt or upset that he or she says negative things to the other. If the person who is attacked responds only to the literal meaning of what was said, any interactions might escalate into a major argument.

On the other hand, if the one who feels attacked can look beyond the superficial meaning into the deeper intent of the words, empathy is possible. Perhaps the friend or partner is hurt, sad, or frustrated, and is expressing those feelings poorly. The attacked person can wonder, "Why is my friend (spouse) talking this way?"

After finding an answer, the attacked person can respond, "I'm sure that you didn't mean what you said, and that something is hurting you a lot. I'd like to understand what I did to make you so upset."

By addressing another person's inner experience, we can resolve our conflicts and deepen our relationships.

## Notes

1. *Menachot* 43b.
2. Ibid.
3. Genesis 14:22, 23.
4. *Bereishit Rabbah* 43:9.
5. Numbers 15:37–41.
6. Tzitzit are made by taking four strands of wool, which are then doubled over to make eight threads. How many of them were blue was a matter of rabbinic debate, ranging from one, two, four, or even eight of the eight strands.
7. *Menachot* 44a.
8. Some Jews in Israel believe that they have definitively identified the *chilazon*, and they use the dye of that fish to produce the blue threads of tzitzit.
9. *Menachot* 43b. That punishment does not apply today since we don't know which fish-dye to use.
10. *Menachot* 43b.
11. Ibid.
12. *Mishnah Avot* 3:1.
13. *Chullin* 89a.
14. *Menachot* 43b.
15. Ibid. 44a.
16. Rashi on Numbers 15:39.
17. Ibid.
18. Genesis 15:5.
19. Rashi on Genesis 15:5.
20. Ibid. 47:28.
21. I Kings 9:3.

22. Numbers, chapters 13 and 14.

23. *Sanhedrin* 67b and *Chullin* 7b.

24. Genesis 14:21.

25. Ibid. 14:23. Abraham's name was actually Abram, but God changed it to Abraham before he fathered Isaac.

26. Ibid.12:2.

27. Ibid. 12:16.

28. *Chullin* 88b.

29. Today, a brother is not allowed to marry his sister-in-law because it is assumed that he won't have the right intentions in so doing. Therefore, *chalitzah* must always be performed if a married man dies childless, has a surviving brother, and the widow wishes to remarry.

30. This is why Moses removed his shoes when he had his first prophetic experience at the burning bush. He had to concentrate totally on spirituality, which necessitated removing his physical connections to the world. They acted as a barrier between himself and God. Prophecy requires divesting oneself of all bodily focus. Removing his shoes allowed Moses to immerse completely in his spiritual experience of God.

    Jewish priests in the Tabernacle and Temple did likewise. They had to take off their shoes and walk barefoot on the cold, stone floors. Today, Jewish priests (*cohanim*) still remove their shoes before blessing the Jewish people because they must be totally connected to the spiritual Source of the blessing.

    My thanks to Rabbi Uziel Milevsky, *zt"l*, for his beautiful exposition of the deeper meaning of *chalitzah*.

31. *Yoma* 86a.

# 13

## Three Levels of Soul

Rabbi Meir asked, "Why was blue selected of all possible colors for the tzitzit? Because the blue reminds us of the color of the ocean, which in turn reminds us of the color of the sky, which then leads us to think about God's Throne,"[1] and His being Master and Creator of the universe.

The Zohar says that every Jew must create a spiritual garment to wear in the next world when his physical garment (the body) is removed. We weave our spiritual garment from the mitzvot that we do while we are in this world.

Our souls have three different levels: *nefesh, ruach,* and *neshamah.* Each level needs a garment to wear in the World to Come. The type of garments that we create parallel the human faculties that we used to make them. Since the *nefesh* is the level of soul that is most identified with the body, the physical acts that we do to perform mitzvot create spiritual garments for it. The *ruach* level of the soul is identified with spirit and speech, and we create its future garments by learning or teaching Torah, by saying kind or comforting words to others, by praying and saying the Shema, and the like. *Neshamah* is the highest level of the soul. The more our thoughts and desires yearn for closeness to God, the more garments we create for it. In other words, we create garments for our three levels of soul with our actions, speech, and thoughts. The three symbolisms in the blue of the tzitzit — the ocean, the heavens, and God's heavenly Throne — remind us to "clothe" each of our three levels of soul.

The "waters of the ocean" represent the physical world. "The heavens" symbolize the giving of the Torah, when the Almighty "descended" from the heavens to Mount Sinai. The Throne of Glory reminds us of God Himself.

The Jews merited these three levels of soul during their early history. A week after their Exodus from Egypt, they crossed the Sea of Reeds. That merited their acquiring the lowest level of soul, the *nefesh*. The Exodus allowed the Jews to become physically free, and the *nefesh* is the only level of soul that requires freedom. *Ruach* and *neshamah* are so exalted that they can never be held captive. The worst that can happen is for us not to be in synchrony with them. When that happens, we can't receive from them, but we can't totally damage their energies, either.[2]

It is possible for us to destroy our *nefesh*'s essence, as well as most of the energies that come from it. This is what happens when a Jew does a sin whose punishment is "*karet*." The Torah says that such a sin causes one's *nefesh* to be cut off. Rabbi Chaim Volozhiner explained that *karet* doesn't mean the entire *nefesh* is cut off, but nine of its ten parts are. In any event, it is the only level of soul that can be "cut off."

God gave Jews access to other parts of the soul during each of three historical events: The Exodus from Egypt freed the *nefesh* from its captivity and enabled it to express itself. Since the pinnacle of that event occurred when the Jews passed through the Sea of Reeds, the blue of the ocean reminds us of the *nefesh*.

The Jews' freedom after the Exodus and their ability to cross the Reed Sea was a divine gift. They did not have to earn it,[3] and they did not yet deserve it when they got it. This event subsequently made it possible for any Jew to become spiritually free at any time, even without doing anything to accomplish it. God's gift of undeserved freedom recurs every year on Passover, when we get spiritual freedom beyond what we deserve.

We often get so mired in sin, or become so complacent, that we could never free ourselves spiritually. God, in His goodness, frees us every Passover according to how we will use that freedom.

The heavens separate the celestial world from our world, and parallel *ruach*. *Ruach* is a level of soul that is higher, and less physically oriented, than *nefesh* is. But it is less purely spiritual than *neshamah*. It is similar to the heavens, which are not as physical as the ocean, yet which rest above the earth.

We acquired *ruach* when God gave us the Torah at Mount Sinai. Just as Torah bridges the gap between the totally physical and the totally spiritual worlds, so does *ruach* stand as a bridge between the *nefesh* and the *neshamah*.

We acquired our *neshamah* when the Jews built the Tabernacle in the desert. This is symbolized by the "waters of heaven." A service called "pouring of the water" took place during the holiday of Tabernacles (Sukkot) when the Tabernacle and Temples stood.

During the year, each of the pilgrimage holidays —

Passover, Shavuot, and Sukkot — allow us to access our respective levels of soul. In ancient times, all male Jews left their homes and made pilgrimages to the Temple in Jerusalem at these times. The purpose of the pilgrimages was to reinforce and nurture each level of our souls. Together, these holidays helped Jews maintain their spiritual health. Strengthening any link in the chain of soul-levels improves our overall spiritual integrity because all three levels are interconnected. For example, anything that improves our *nefesh* or *ruach* makes the garment of *neshamah* that much more accessible.

## The Contribution of Each Holiday

*Nefesh* has ten links, the highest of which connects to the lowest link of *ruach*. The top link of *ruach* connects to the lowest link of *neshamah*. Thus, the stronger the lower links, the more they strengthen the higher ones, and our connection to God Himself.

When Jews went to the Temple on Passover, they strengthened their *nefesh*. When we celebrate Passover today, it still helps us renew our connection to *nefesh*. When we celebrate the giving of the Torah on the holiday of Shavuot (the Feast of Weeks), it strengthens our *ruach*. We move out of our physical homes and live in God's spiritual dwelling on Sukkot, the holiday of Tabernacles. That allows us to be engulfed by our *neshamah*.

In ancient times, Jews celebrated these pilgrimage holidays at the Tabernacle or Temple "before God." The entire purpose of these holidays was to feed each of the soul's levels and reinforce God's reality to every Jew.

Today, if our *nefesh* goes into captivity, we can again

become worthy of accessing it every Passover. Celebrating the holiday of Shavuot helps us build a foundation for our *ruach*. Observing the holiday of Sukkot aids us in making garments for our *neshamah*. Thus, every pilgrimage holiday can help us make spiritual garments. By the time God divests us of our physical ones, we will hopefully have taken them off long before.

Rabbi Moshe Chaim Luzzatto said that accepting the Torah gave us only the *ruach* level of soul, whereas the holiday of Tabernacles gave us access to our soul's highest level, our *neshamah*. Inasmuch as we usually think that receiving the Torah brought us to our spiritual peak, we would expect Shavuot to have given us access to *neshamah*, not to *ruach*. How, then, do we understand Rabbi Luzzatto's comment?

While it is true that getting the Torah gave us our greatest ability to function in this world, the power of repentance, symbolized by the Tabernacle, is so great that it reaches God's Throne of Glory. This means that when a Jew yearns to rekindle a relationship with the One Above, he or she can reach into their *neshamah* and do this.

The Jews could have gained access to their *neshamot* simply by following the Torah, but that would have taken a very long time. Proper repentance (*teshuvah*) lets us shed our old self and assume a new identity. We can use that to reach the level of *neshamah* much quicker than using other means.

## Moses and Aaron

Moses' primary role vis-à-vis the Jewish people was to teach them Torah. This is why he represented the soul-level of *ruach*, from which people could grow to the level of *neshamah*. His brother Aaron represented the Jews' ability to reach the level of *neshamah* via sincere repentance.

When Moses was on Mount Sinai receiving the Ten Commandments, the Jews thought that he was never coming back. They wanted Aaron to make them a "leader" to replace Moses, so Aaron suggested what he hoped would be a delaying tactic until Moses returned. Unfortunately, his plan backfired, and Aaron ended up making a golden calf. Despite his good intentions, he acknowledged his culpability for the fact that the calf was made.

From that point on, he became a symbol of repentance. He repented so thoroughly for his misdeed that he caused degrees of repentance to be accessible to the entire Jewish people. Going through his personal process of repentance inspired the whole nation to simultaneously do the same. They also benefitted from his repentance because they achieved a more elevated relationship with God by virtue of their connection with Aaron. "Spiritual osmosis" allowed them to benefit from their leader's repentance.

When the Jews saw how deeply Aaron regretted his sin, they felt that they must certainly repent for their misdeed. His deep yearning to return to God allowed those who were connected to him to benefit unconsciously from his actions. Aaron repented not only to wipe clean his personal slate, but to undo the damage that he had caused the entire Jewish nation. That elevated anyone who was connected to him.

The gifts that the Jews received in their leaders' merits reflected what Moses and Aaron represented. Moses' merits caused manna to come from heaven, which fed the Israelites for forty years in the wilderness. This Heavenly gift symbolized the soul-level of *ruach* and Torah-learning, which were Moses' hallmarks.

Aaron's merit brought the Israelites heavenly protective clouds. They symbolized the *neshamah's* garments.

## Exchanging Garments

God must "peel" off a deceased person's garments if his essence is inseparable from his body. When we spend our lives preparing spiritual garments for the future, we need only exchange our garment from this world for a different one in the afterlife. If we spend our lives performing mitzvot, learning Torah, and dedicating our thoughts and desires to God, we are not held captive in our physical garments. Our spiritual deeds and thoughts allow us to wear a more suitable garment when the appropriate time comes.

Tzitzit remind us to spend our lives preparing spiritual garments so that our physical ones never get too close to our skin. We should never reach a point where we can't take off our garments of this world.

In this sense, garments symbolize freedom, which is why tzitzit are so closely associated with the Exodus from Egypt. The last paragraph of the Shema speaks about tzitzit, then about the Exodus. Tzitzit represent spiritual garments that we cannot wear unless we are free to take off the physical garment we already have on. We don't wear one suit on top of another. We only wear a second set of clothes after taking off the first one. Tzitzit help free us from our physical garments so that we can put on spiritual clothing.

The Torah illustrates this with the story of Joseph.[4] He was challenged by a most difficult moral test when he ran his Egyptian master's household. The master's wife was in love with Joseph. One day, she almost succeeded in seducing him, but a moment before succumbing, Joseph saw his father Jacob's image.[5]

The Sfat Emmet says that "his father's image" meant that Joseph saw the "clothes" that Jacob had made during his lifetime. Jacob had devoted his life to weaving spiritual garments for himself instead of identifying with his physical garment.

Joseph did not visualize Jacob's physical appearance. He saw Jacob's spiritual garb in an exquisitely timely revelation. The moment that Joseph verged on succumbing to physical temptation, he saw that he must not identify with his body and instead devote himself to his soul's needs. When Joseph saw his father's "image," he asked himself what kind of soul-garment he would weave if he committed adultery. That convinced him to run away from his temptress.

The Torah says that his master's wife grabbed Joseph's garment when he escaped. He wrestled loose, leaving it in her hands.[6] This means that Joseph understood the message of his father's garment and decided not to be trapped in his superficial clothes (his physical desires). He left them in the woman's clutches.

This also explains the earlier story about the Jew who visited the prostitute. Before he could sin with her, his tzitzit struck him in the face. That made him realize what he was doing and motivated him to resist the temptation. What the tzitzit really did were to remind him not to make into something substantial what was intended only to be a garment. When he thought about his intended act from that perspective, he couldn't bring himself to sin.

## Faith in a Mitzvah

We are told to "have faith in God," or "have faith" in ourselves, but there is also a concept of believing in the effects of a mitzvah. After discussing the laws of the Day of Atonement (Yom Kippur), Rabbi Moshe Isserles said that repentance only changes us if we believe that it does.

A mitzvah can only draw spiritual light into us if we believe in its power, and we must be capable of receiving what it has to offer. Believing in a mitzvah opens our inner spiritual channels and allows the mitzvah to affect us.

If a man wants to grow morally, he can start by wearing tzitzit, being careful to observe the mitzvah with all of its particulars. If he says, "I know myself. Wearing tzitzit won't help me be more moral," he will be right. He must have faith in what the mitzvah can accomplish in order for it to work.

Having faith in a mitzvah without making any other changes will also not do much to improve one's morality. But believing in a mitzvah's power lets us draw on the spiritual energies that become available to us when we do an act. That gives us more potential for growth, whether or not we are aware of it.

When a man wears tefillin, he can also want it to affect him. Once he believes in its power, things start to change.

Rather than being burdens, mitzvot are the exact tools that we need to help us grow from our challenges. Neglecting mitzvot never helps us to be on better terms with God, because they are the support system that allows us to transcend our limitations.

## Notes

1. *Menachot* 43b.

2. This is one opinion. Rabbi Luzzatto, in *The Way of God* I:3–4, says that we *can* destroy the *neshamah*.

3. However, Nachshon ben Aminadav showed his faith by being willing to enter the waters up to his neck before they parted.

4. Genesis 39:1–19.

5. *Sotah* 36b.

6. Genesis 39:12, 13.

# 14

# The Blessings before the Shema

Jewish prayer services are very structured. Every morning, we say a series of blessings, followed by psalms that praise God. Then the prayer leader of a quorum of men calls them to worship. That is followed by two blessings, the Shema, a third blessing, and then the Eighteen Benedictions (known as the *Shemoneh Esrei* or *Amidah*). The *Amidah* is the central Jewish prayer.

The evening service has a similar structure. It begins with a call to worship, followed by two blessings, the Shema, two more blessings, and then the *Amidah*.

Following are the first blessing and prayers that precede the Shema in the morning service:

Blessed are You, Lord our God, King of the world, who forms light and creates darkness, makes peace and creates everything.[1]

The One who brings light to the earth, and to those who live upon it, with compassion, and in His goodness renews every day, constantly, the act of Creation. How great are Your deeds, Lord, You made them all with wisdom, the earth is full of Your possessions. The King who is elevated alone since yore, who is praised, glorified, and exalted from days of old. Eternal God, with Your great compassion have compassion on us; Master of our power, Rock of our strength, Shield of our salvation, be a strength for us. God of blessing, great in knowledge, who prepared and worked on the rays of the sun. The Good One formed honor for His Name, He surrounded His power with luminaries. The leaders of His hosts are holy ones who elevate the Almighty. They always tell of the honor of God and His holiness. Be a source of blessing, Lord our God, above the praise of the works of Your hands, and above the luminaries that You made. They should glorify You forever....

To the God of blessing, they will give pleasant (songs), to the King, living and existing God, they will say songs and make praises heard. Because He alone does mighty deeds, makes new things, is Master of wars, sows righteousness, makes salvations sprout, creates cures, is awesome for praises, Master of wonders. He renews, in His goodness, daily, constantly, the act of Creation. As it is said: "To the One who makes the great lights, because His kindness is eternal."[2] Shine a new light on Zion, and let us quickly be worthy of its light. Blessed are You, Lord, Who forms the luminaries.

These verses describe how God constantly preserves and renews His creation of the universe.

The blessing that follows the one above alludes to God's renewal of the Jewish people. We represent the human beings that He most "counts on." That blessing says:

With great love You have loved us, Lord our God, with great and abundant pity You have pitied us. Our Father, our King, for the sake of our forefathers who trusted You, and to whom You taught the laws of life, likewise be gracious to us and teach us. Our Father, the Merciful Father who bestows mercy, have mercy on us, and give our hearts the ability to understand and fathom, to listen, to learn and to teach, to guard, to do, and to observe all of the words of Your Torah's teaching with love. Enlighten our eyes with Your Torah, and make our hearts cling to Your commandments, and unify our hearts to love and fear Your Name, and let us never be embarrassed forever. Because we have trusted in Your holy, great, and awesome Name, we will rejoice and be happy with Your salvation. Bring us in peace from the four corners of the earth, and lead us upright to our land. For You are a God who makes salvation happen, and You chose us from every nation and people. You brought us close to Your great Name forever, in truth, in order to thank You and express Your unity with love. Blessed are You, Lord, Who chooses His people Israel with love.

There are two primary ways of discovering God's existence: one is by contemplating the order and complexity of the universe and its component parts. When we do that, we marvel at its grandeur and intricacy. That prompts us to realize that the world could only be here due to a deliberate act of creation by an infinitely wise Being.

Scientific evidence also supports a Big Bang theory. It states that at one time, no matter existed, and then it instantly did. If the universe's components did not exist at one time, then suddenly came into being, it follows that a Creator, who Himself was not material and did not need to be created, made that happen.

The orderliness of the universe, and the exquisite timeliness of various events that allowed human and animal life to exist on earth also bespeak a Creator's handiwork. The primitive life forms that initially came into being could never have evolved on their own into the complex life forms that are here today. In addition, the intricate ecosystems and workings of nature proclaim an intelligent Creator who put a magnificent plan into action, not random forces at work.[3]

This is the message of the first blessing that precedes the Shema. The purpose of the Shema is to proclaim that God is One, but it only makes sense to do that if we believe in God altogether! How do we know that He exists? The first blessing after the Shema tells us to look at His handiwork — the galaxies, our solar system, the functioning of nature — and we will know that such an amazing, dynamic entity had to be brought here by a Composer and Orchestrator.

The second blessing before the Shema reminds us of another way to know that God exists — by learning Torah. Torah teaches us that God revealed Himself to the entire Jewish people when He gave us His book over 3,300 years ago. Since then, our people have faithfully transmitted our knowledge of God, and His will for us, from generation to generation. We have only to study Torah to remind ourselves of the reality of the One Above.[4]

The first blessing before the Shema praises the Master of the World for renewing the universe every day.[5] The second blessing praises His love for, and constant renewal of, His people Israel through our connection to Torah. He continually bonds with us in a way that brings us closer to His service, and we ask Him to continue to show us love and allow us to teach and learn Torah. We thank Him for renewing us in a unique way every day as we actualize our individual potentials through Torah. Since people are the main focus and reason for creating the universe, God renews every Jew daily.

Since studying Torah allows us to discover new perspectives about ourselves, new feelings, new insights, and new values, before we say Shema we ask God to help us understand and transmit Torah, and perform its mitzvot.

Although the Almighty constantly renews the universe, we still ask for our personal gift of renewal, since our choices are independent of the world's renewal. God renews nature every day, without the earth making a decision to revolve, without trees choosing to send out leaves, without flowers choosing to bloom, and so on. In a sense, nature gets renewed as part of a universal "law."

This is not true for people, though. Our quality of existence and personal renewal depends upon our choices. Our greatness lies is our ability to choose. How much of our potential renewal we actualize depends upon how we choose to live. We can make new choices every day that express our uniqueness as human beings, especially through learning Torah.

God constantly renews each part of His world after "deciding" whether or not it should be maintained. He literally re-creates the world every day by putting various blessings into it. For example, He may give someone a special opportunity to do a mitzvah of lovingkindness today. Tomorrow, that person might get a chance to grow spiritually by seeing God's Hand in his financial life. The day after, he may have a chance to honor the Sabbath by buying a food that he really likes, which is not normally available. God creates each day anew for the specific spiritual opportunity that it presents. The qualitative changes that we bring to the world, and to ourselves, contribute to our spiritual growth and to the world's spiritual rectification every day.

To this end, we need to make use of the unique potentials

and energy that every day contains. Every day gives us new opportunities to grow spiritually by accomplishing goals that only appear that day.

This also happens with respect to learning Torah. We make Torah new by learning insights today that we didn't know yesterday. We need to learn Torah in a way that it always reveals new perspectives, new ideas, and new factual information to us, even if we have studied it many times, from many angles. It should continually give us deeper insights into doing mitzvot, which we then apply to how we live and feel. We need to learn Torah with enough depth and commitment to find new things in it today that we didn't know yesterday.

The author once gave a talk about prayer in a certain community. Four years later she gave the same talk to a different group of people there. She tried to dissuade one man who had previously heard her from attending, but he came anyway. After she concluded her talk, the man told her how much he enjoyed hearing her.

"But didn't you remember the talk from before?" she asked.

"As a matter of fact, I did," he replied, "but I still enjoyed it. You see, your words were similar both times, but I have changed a lot these past four years. What I heard, and the way I understood it now, was very different from the last time I heard you."

Torah's beauty is that it is limitless. Even relearning the same information can give us new insights, or help us see things with renewed relevance. Since we don't always know what spiritual opportunities are present each day, our new insights into Torah can always be that day's opportunity. We become new people every day by using each day's infusion of blessing and energy to sensitize us to the ongoing novelty of life.

Research has shown that where people learn is very important. Learning in a place that is boring and static makes it hard to relate to new material, because we associate that boring environment with the information. Changing the scenery can open us up to new ideas and feelings. The Almighty puts a "change of pace" into every unit of time as one of His many gifts to us so that life need never be stale.

In the Shema, we agree to uphold God's government. If Judaism once excited us, but we haven't felt that way in years, we are simply living an old commitment. That way of living is not pledging the kind of responsibility to God's government that He wants from us.

Accepting the "yoke of heaven" means that we commit ourselves to Judaism anew every day. That requires more than having deeper Torah insights. It means renewing our relationship to God when we wake up every morning. We must decide whether or not having a relationship with our Creator is worthwhile every day, not rest on the laurels of a commitment that we made years ago.

That is why we precede the Shema by saying that God puts novelty into the universe and into Torah. We use these universal and personal ways of rejuvenating ourselves to renew our commitment to God when we say the Shema. Both types of renewal exist so that we will use them in our relationship with our Creator.

Thinking about God's renewal of the world helps us appreciate His omnipotence and the fact that He makes miracles because He cares about what happens to His world. When we learn Torah, we know that our personal renewal could only come about through God's connection to Torah and us. Someone who doesn't study Torah may not see the constant, divine providence over the world. Such a person sees the world's renewal as merely nature or evolution at work. We need a higher level of understanding to recognize that nature is renewed by a Supreme Power.

As we renew our relationship with our Creator, we reveal His Presence in the world more and more. Torah helps us identify the Source of universal existence and renewal, while it moves us closer to Him. The more we do this, the more we bring our Creator here in a way that He wasn't here before. The more we absorb His new gift to us every day, the more we bring the divine Presence out of "hiding."

## Notes

1. The original verse was from Isaiah 45:7, and ended, "...makes peace and creates evil." This ties into the earlier idea that evil was a necessary and important part of Creation.

2. Psalms 136:7.

3. An excellent explanation of the Torah's depiction of the origin of the universe and life on earth in light of modern scientific knowledge is found in Nathan Aviezer's *In the Beginning: Biblical Creation and Science* (Hoboken, N.J.: Ktav, 1990).

4. Psalm 19 alludes to these two ways of finding God. It begins, "The heavens tell the story of the glory of God, and the firmament speaks of the work of Your hands."

   After discussing the revelation of God through nature in the next few verses, the psalm continues, "The Torah of the Lord is perfect, restoring the soul...."

5. These concepts are discussed in *The Way of God* 4:4:11.

# 15

## The Blessing after the Shema

Shortly after the Shema we say:

You are the help of our forefathers forever, a Shield and Savior to their descendants in every generation. Your dwelling place is at the top of the world, and Your justice and Your righteousness go to the ends of the earth. Happy is the man who listens to Your commandments, and who puts Your Torah and Your words on his heart. It is true that You are the Master of Your nation, and a mighty King to fight their battles. It is true that You are first, and You are last, and apart from You we have no King who is a Redeemer and Savior. You redeemed us from Egypt, Lord our God, and freed us from a house of slaves. You killed all of their firstborn and redeemed our firstborn. You split the Reed Sea, and drowned their deliberate sinners, and the dear ones [Israel] You brought across; You covered their tormentors [the Egyptians] with water — not one of them remained. For this reason the loved ones praised and exalted God, and the dear ones gave hymns, songs, and praises, blessings and thanks to the King, living and existing God. He is exalted and elevated, great and awesome. He lowers the arrogant and raises the lowly, draws out captives and frees the humble, helps the destitute, and answers His people at the time they cry to Him....

This prayer describes some of the miracles that God did for us as a nation during and after the Exodus from Egypt. This reminds us that the world does not function in two distinct ways, one of which follows the laws of nature, with its constant renewal, and the other of which governs how people function and are renewed. These two orders of existence are really one and the same.

One problem that we have to contend with is boredom. Everything material becomes stale as we get used to it over time. But time is a divine creation that only exists in this world. If we transcend this world, there is no concept of time. In spiritual realms, past, present, and future are one and the same. We can only get bored in the confines of the physical world, never in the spiritual world.[1]

By definition, spirituality has no limits, which is one reason why spiritual realms are referred to as *chai olamim* — "eternal life." Spiritual life is constantly vibrant and exciting. Boredom is only possible within the captivity of materialism.

The two paragraphs preceding the Shema express our exhilaration at God's renewal of the world. We thank Him for injecting it with novelty so that we don't get bored. He refreshes all of creation by connecting it to His own spirituality. His eternal life force energizes it. The more anything connects to its Source, the more life it has.

Some spiritual people have tremendous energy, with no physical explanation for it. This is because they are connected to a Source that doesn't tire. Many people have seen rabbis or teachers who look sickly and tired when they walk into a room. Minutes later, they give a Torah lecture, and their years, frailty, and fatigue seem to melt away. People who are very connected to Torah can be so invigorated by it that they seem ageless.

Torah is so tied to the Source of life that we even call it "the tree of life." It always has new things in it since it is connected to Him.

The blessing after the Shema refers to miracles. Lest we think that nature and the spiritual world are totally separate, this blessing teaches us that the mundane physical world, and its miracles, are merely God's ways of manifesting His presence. Without His interventions, nature could not change so that miracles occur.

After the Shema, we say that nature is nurtured by its Source, and His miracles help us see that. Saying the Shema sensitizes us to how God's personal connections to us apply to the world at large.

One beautiful effect of saying the Shema is that it reveals God to us. The more we come to appreciate our Creator's unity when we say the Shema, the more we see how miracles manifest His Presence in nature.

The more we see God in the world, the less we "believe" in the laws of nature. People who can make miracles are able to see what is real and hidden, instead of what is apparent. They know that the One who makes the laws of nature can change them at will.

The Talmud tells a story about Rabbi Chanina ben Dosa who was extraordinarily poor. One Sabbath eve, he didn't have enough money to buy oil for the Sabbath lamps. He asked his daughter what they had in the house, and she replied, "Vinegar."

He responded, "Let the One who makes oil burn make vinegar burn." She filled the lamps with vinegar, lit them, and they burned until the next night.[2] As far as the rabbi was concerned, the One who made the laws of nature could change them at will, and that is exactly what happened.

When we take potentials for renewal (the first two blessings), and use them in our relationship with God (the Shema), we can appreciate miracles or even make them happen (the blessing that follows the Shema.)

Inasmuch as the themes of the prayers surrounding the Shema are about renewal, the Shema should really be said in the morning. After all, that is when the entire world, and we, wake up. We also tend to appreciate the gift of renewal most during the day. But since nighttime rounds out and completes this process, we repeat the blessings with the Shema at night.[3]

Obviously, the completion of renewal (at night) is not as significant as the daytime process. That is why the nighttime blessings of renewal are shorter than those of the morning. The process no longer occurs at night, it simply ends.[4]

Besides saying the Shema every morning and evening, we also say it just before going to sleep. This is unrelated to the biblical and rabbinic commandments to read the Shema. We say it at bedtime because it grants us spiritual protection.[5] We draw away from higher spiritual levels when we sleep, which is why the Talmud calls sleep one-sixtieth of death. The Shema protects us at those times, similar to the way mezuzot protect us.

If we say the entire Shema after nightfall, we must only repeat its first two verses and first paragraph before we go to sleep. If we haven't said the evening Shema in its proper time, we must say all three paragraphs before going to sleep.

Before we say the bedtime Shema, it is customary to forgive anyone who might have hurt us that day and not bear a grudge against him or her. This helps protect us at night, and enables us to start the next day with a clean slate.

## Notes

1. This is one opinion. Some commentators state that souls have continual spiritual growth in the afterlife. Without it, they would get bored.

2. *Taanit* 25a.

3. *The Way of God* 4:4:12. When we go to sleep at night, we don't work to elevate our souls. However, parts of the soul leave the body and have access to higher spiritual realms than they had during the day.

4. *The Way of God* 4:4:12.

5. *Berachot* 5a.